CHOICES Gift from God

CHOICES Gift from God

By

P.I. Tampke

Prologue

Hey there, adventurous soul!

Welcome, dear reader, to a world bursting with excitement and wonder! You've just crossed the threshold into a realm where imagination dances and possibilities abound. Picture this: a late-night brainstorming session, caffeine-fueled and full of wild ideas, where the initial flicker of inspiration struck like lightning. That was the moment I knew I had to channel this whirlwind of thoughts into something exciting, resonant, and utterly unmissable. It's a cascade of creativity that has led us right here—to the pages of this book!

As I ventured through research, diving headfirst into a treasure trove of stories, facts, and personal anecdotes, the tapestry began to weave itself together. Every twist and turn fueled my passion and curiosity, compelling me to dig deeper and ask, "What makes a story unforgettable?" It was an exhilarating quest filled with laughs, surprises, and perhaps a few late-night existential crises. This book reflects that journey—a fusion of insights and inspiration, crafted with love and a dash of craziness.

So, why this topic, you might ask? It's simple. We, as humans, crave connection, exploration, and a sprinkle of magic in our lives. It's not just about understanding the narrative; it's about feeling it, living it. I wanted to capture that visceral experience and share it with you. Each chapter is a stepping stone, bridging insights to ignite your imagination and challenge the norm.

And oh! The incredible people I met along the way. From experts enlightening me with their wisdom to everyday folks sharing their extraordinary journeys, their stories embedded themselves within the text. This book is a celebration of their voices, showing that each person carries a richness of experience worth illuminating.

Now, hold on tight! We're about to embark on an exhilarating roller coaster of ideas and revelations. It's a wild ride, with peaks that'll make your heart race and valleys where you'll catch your breath in awe. I promise, by the end, you'll emerge not just a reader, but an adventurer transformed by the exploration of new realms of thought.

I encourage you to dive in, state your mind, let the words resonate, and feel the energy as you turn each page. Take your time—savor every sentence, every twist. This isn't just a book; it's an invitation to rediscover your sense of wonder. Whether you're reading this under a blanket, on a sunny day in a park, or during a cozy café visit, soak in the experience!

As you navigate through the chapters, I hope you'll find moments where you nod, laugh, or perhaps even pause and reflect. That's the magic I'm hoping to spark—a synergy between your heart and these words. Immerse yourself, engage with the content, and allow it to challenge your perspective.

I can't wait for you to uncover the insights lurking beneath the surface. They're bold, daring, and sometimes slightly mischievous! So, keep an open heart and an adventurous spirit. This story is alive, and it begs to be shared and lived. Thank you for joining me on this incredible quest. It's going to be quite the adventure, and I'm thrilled to share it with you.

So, go ahead, grab that cup of your favorite brew, snuggle up, and let's dive into this explosive journey together! Keep turning the pages—the best is yet to come. I promise you, we're just getting started.

With an adventurous heart,

P.I. Tampke

Dedication

I would like to dedicate this book to my Earthly Father in Heaven, **_William Albert Tampke_**, And My **_Heavenly Father_** who is my **_Lord and Savior_**. Without my Fathers I would have nothing…

Acknowledgement

CHOICE was the word I received from God. God often in my life gives me a word and always prophetic. When I first heard the word CHOICE I was in awe. I had lived my life not realizing my life was the journey of CHOICES. When God created Adam and Eve he gave them the gift of CHOICE. They were given the ability to CHOOSE!!! We all know how their *CHOICES* have Rippled through eternity.

I sincerely pray as you read through this journey of CHOICES you may be blessed and to CHOOSE

God and he will lead you down the path of Gifted CHOICES.

Table of Contents

The Dawn of CHOICE

The First Breath

The world echoed with a symphony of new beginnings, as the first breath reverberated through the air like a gentle whisper. In that sacred instant, a delicate life emerged fragile yet unstoppable force, ready to embark on its journey through a complex labyrinth of CHOICES. The moment of birth stands as a transcendent gateway, where the immensity of existence meets the simplicity of a single, life-giving intake of air. At the threshold of this monumental entrance, it is here that

CHOICE first tiptoes onto the stage, unnoticed but undeniably present.

Imagine the scene: soft lights, tender sounds, and the unmistakable scent of potential hang in the atmosphere. A newborn lie ensconced in a cocoon of warmth, casting their first gaze upon a world that twinkles with possibility. In that blink, awareness begins to bloom. Each aspect of the surroundings becomes more real, more vibrant. It is as if life itself has tapped the baby's shoulder, urging them to awaken from a state of unknowing bliss. And yet, though they cannot comprehend the enormity of this awakening, they are already wrapped in the folds of CHOICE.

Breath by breath, each inhale constructs an existence, each exhale a silent testament to the CHOICE inherent within life. Each newborn is a canvas, blank yet brimming with colors waiting to merge and dance in unpredictable ways. What shape will their story take? What hues will paint their experiences? The taint of innocence rides alongside knowledge, and the crux of CHOICE is born in this dichotomy. At this stage, without the burdens of complex decision-making, life is simply an exploration, an adventure of the senses.

The canvas is tantalizingly expansive. No judgments clutter

the fresh strokes of experience. The newborn knows the comfort of a mother's embrace, hears the softness of a lullaby, and tastes the sweetness of a smile shared. Each interaction begins to etch the contours of their understanding, laying the foundational blocks of identity. If only we could understand the gravity of this moment and the depth of the CHOICES it holds, and we'd cherish our first breath even more fiercely.

The journey of CHOICE for the newborn is a gradual awakening rather than an immediate realization. It begins in subtlety—the CHOICE to grasp a finger that offers comfort, the instinct to cry for nourishment, or the quiet learnings that take place by observing their surroundings. In these formative moments, the essence of CHOICE is revealed not through grand decisions but through instinctual responses—reactions to comfort, warmth, and love. The first CHOICE arrives in the form of a connection. A gentle squeeze of tiny fingers wraps around the hope and protection extended by a caring hand. Suddenly, the world does not seem so vast; it feels intimate and warm.

The family plays a critical role in this initial awakening. Every laugh, each fulfilled need, and every lesson imparted weave together to create a nurturing tapestry that will guide the child through subsequent CHOICES. The echoes of laughter cradle them; the tone of voices in their environment shapes their perceptions long before virtue and discernment enter the picture. A mother's singing voice becomes a lullaby—a link to love and safety. A father's laughter becomes an anchor, holding them firm in the storm of uncertainties that lie ahead. In this context, CHOICE transcends mere decision-making; it transforms into a dance of influences, woven by the threads of family dynamics, culture, and environment.

As the child grows, this nascent awareness blossoms into something far richer. The once-blank canvas begins to fill, strokes of CHOICE expanding with nearly every new experience. The child's laughter sings through the air as they take their first steps, a heavy moment with CHOICE. There's joy in learning to walk and a hint of fear in the unknown— each trembling step founded upon an inherent CHOICE to explore. A new realm greets them, vibrant with possibilities and laden with the implicit answers to unasked questions. How will they navigate this world? The initial instinctual CHOICES evolve into exploratory ones, filled with the thrill of possibility.

Innocence sprinkled with daring curiosity propels the infant through formative years, creating a mosaic of experiences that establish the foundation of their worldview. These years are imbued with the purest essence of CHOICE. Children begin asserting autonomy—picking a favorite toy, choosing whom to share it with, deciding to venture into another room. With each CHOICE, they perform a delicate balancing act, weighing desires against the fears of disappointment or rejection.

As they learn, they question—"Why?" becomes a favorite word. They navigate their relationships with the world around them, eager to process their preferences while harmonizing them with family values. Herein lies a profound dichotomy: children are guided by instinct and affection but remain tethered to the CHOICES modeled by those they love and admire. Parents' reactions and the subtle nuances of those early CHOICES inform deeper instincts about what is right or wrong—what is safe and what is frightening.

As CHOICES become increasingly complex, children learn the ramifications of their decisions. A forgotten apology, a delayed acknowledgement of a friend, or even moments of embarrassing forgetfulness transform simple CHOICES into greater life lessons. They absorb the reactions of others like sponges, processing the emotions that follow the consequences of their actions. In this way, each CHOICE made becomes a steppingstone, creating a deeper understanding of not merely how to choose, but how those CHOICES intertwine with the lives of others.

Reflecting on our own beginnings, we might find ourselves filled with nostalgia and wistfulness, remembering the simplicity of our early stages—the first breath, the tactile sensations of being cradled, the warmth of touch. We often romanticize these moments, veiling them in a mist of sepia-toned imagination. Yet, within that softness lies the profound reality of life's first CHOICES. We begin to see the connections between our journey and that of every being on this earth. The CHOICES we made, even if not fully conscious at the time, set forth ripples that have the potential to influence others.

A mother held me close during my first moments; her heartbeat resonated with mine. I was blessed with the quiet safety of her arms. In that moment, I felt cherished. As I grew, I became aware of the CHOICES we all encounter. Each moment struck notes of excitement, fear, joy, and uncertainty. The CHOICES shaped me, molded my character, and aligned my values with the world. I often wonder how many lives were altered simply by taking that first breath and allowing that moment to unfold.

The power of CHOICE glimmers like sunlight on a rippling lake, and our early experiences often echo throughout our narratives, intertwining in ways we may not fully understand.

The CHOICES we made as children create ripples that extend well beyond our immediate experiences.

The canvas continues to fill as we evolve, as we paint details influenced by ever-changing environments and the CHOICES others make around us. Extended family gatherings become lively venues where love and acceptance blossom alongside tensions and misunderstandings. Workplaces shape our destinies through CHOICES each person encounters daily—decisions that can spiral into opportunities or setbacks, defining who we become.

Our perspectives build from the CHOICES made at every step. Reflection allows us to ponder not just our beginnings, but the interwoven complexities of existence. The CHOICES made during childhood, while often perceived as trivial, frame how we perceive ourselves and interact with those around us. The interplay of light and shadow manifests through every decision, shaping who we are destined to be.

As we look at our lives through a more seasoned lens, possibilities reflect upon the countless CHOICES faced over the years. What if the CHOICE to play with one friend over another had lasting implications? What if the decision to pursue art instead of science shaped our future careers? Each

CHOICE, seemingly small in isolation, can lead to fractals of significance, stretching into vast unknowns. The fragile web of life spins continuously, intersecting and diverging through each decision.

In this exploration of life CHOICES stemming from the very first breath, we uncover the essence of being human—the sacred gift of CHOICE bestowed upon us by virtue of existence itself. We learn that CHOICE is a responsibility, interwoven within the backdrop of family and communal life. It beckons us to embrace awareness, freeing us to analyze not just our actions, but the consequences they may herald.

Every breath taken becomes a metaphorical palette, prolonging life's artistry. The canvas remains malleable; every moment involves selecting a color, sketching out new patterns, and risking the smear of brushes upon that sacred surface. As we navigate through the labyrinth of existence, we become ever aware of our sacred role within the larger narrative of life. Our CHOICES echo through the corridors of time, intertwined with the CHOICES made by those preceding us— ancestors whose breaths linger on in the tapestry of collective existence.

In conclusion, the first breath signifies the dawn of limitless

CHOICES. Universes of possibility unfurl from where we stand today, shaped with every breath that follows. The magnificence of CHOICE can sometimes feel overwhelming, yet it also imbues our existence with remarkable depth. It reminds us that from the moment we take that first breath, we are not just passive participants in life's story; we are dynamic creators shaping the very fabric of our destinies. Yes, the weight of CHOICE may remain with us, but so too does the joy that emerges in the act of choosing. The believers, dreamers, and stewards of tomorrow await the CHOICES we will make today, laced with the wisdom gleaned from the sacredness of each breath we've taken.

Innocence and Potential

In the tender embrace of early childhood, life is a mesmerizing tapestry of innocence and boundless potential. Each moment holds an exquisite promise, as little ones dance through days of wonder, their laughter echoing against the backdrop of curiosity. The formative years of life are like a beautiful garden, where parents sow dreams, tend them with hope, and water them with love. Every smile and tear weaves together a delicate narrative, wrapping around the heart with unspoken truths about who we are and who we may become.

Parents, those intricate architects of futures, often gaze lovingly at their children, casting visions upon them like stars sprinkled across a midnight sky. Each child becomes a canvas, waiting for the vibrant colors of experiences to be brushed onto their lives. They envision their little ones soaring through life with the wings of ambition, embarking on adventures that will shape their destinies. These dreams, however, are not merely fantasies; they are sparks igniting the imaginations of both parent and child, illuminating the path ahead.

Within this parent-child dynamic lies a powerful exchange of hopes and fears. Parents nurture aspirations, wanting their children to embody the dreams they hold dear. Perhaps there is the earnest desire for a daughter to become a doctor, a son to be an artist, or a child to dance freely without limits. This transference of desires paints early CHOICES with vibrant hues, imbuing the child with a sense of possibilities that radiate outward like ripples on a pond. Yet, in this process of dreaming, there exists a duality—an intertwining of encouragement and limitation, hopes and fears. Parents may unconsciously project their own aspirations onto their children, shaping their perceptions of what is attainable or, conversely, what lies beyond reach.

Imagine the innocent eyes of a young girl, alight with

wonder as she twirls in her favorite dress. In her world, she is not bound by constraints but is instead buoyed by endless possibilities. As the sun filters through her bedroom window, she dreams of traveling to far-off lands, exploring vast oceans, and singing before adoring crowds. Within those fleeting moments, we find the essence of potential unfurling—a flower blooming spontaneously in the warm embrace of sunlight. Each spin tells a story, a tapestry of dreams woven together in her heart.

Yet, it is important to recognize that this journey of exploration is not without its shadows. The very same parent who dreams of their child becoming a doctor may, through the lens of anxiety, inadvertently convey the fear of failure or the weight of expectations. The lush garden of potential can sprout thorns, where miscommunications and fears coalesce and foster a sense of apprehension in the child. The girl in her dress may begin to feel the tug of societal expectations, a whisper of doubt subtly creeping in, warning her that becoming an adventurer may not be practical or responsible. And as she grows, those whispers may manifest into self-doubt, causing her to revisit her long-held dreams and perhaps choose to abandon them altogether.

In sharing these reflections, it is vital to consider how these familial dynamics shape our early CHOICES. The narrative threads of our childhood are complex, intricately laced with joys and challenges. They offer insight into how children perceive the world around them. Readers are invited to pause and reflect upon their own experiences—what dreams were woven into the fabric of their youth? Were they nourished in an environment of encouragement, or did they encounter the veils of limitation that directed their pathways?

Look again at the small child spinning in her dress, absorbed in the rhythm of imagination. She ventures into a realm where nothing feels impossible. The very act of playing—a simple exploration of self—encourages a natural curiosity and instinctual learning that serves as the bedrock for adulthood. It is in this space of unrestrained exploration that foundational CHOICES arise. Should she climb that tree, venture into the unknown, or build a fort out of pillows? Each little CHOICE—nuanced yet monumental—pushes the boundaries of her existence and transforms her reality.

As she grows, the world around her introduces more complexity. School walls envelop her, and new relationships form—a dance of connections filled with laughter and tears. In this social microcosm, she learns to navigate the intricate network of friendships and rivalries that shape identity. Here, there is fertile ground for CHOICES to bloom: the way she responds to friendship dilemmas, the challenges found in learning environments, and the simple act of sharing or standing up for herself. Children's CHOICES may seem small in the grand narrative of adulthood, but they lay the cornerstone for future decisions—CHOICES that can echo throughout their lives.

Through each experience, a child learns resilience, an invaluable gift. When faced with disappointment, joy, or challenge, they encounter CHOICES that shape their perspectives. The little girl may perceive a setback as a failure—or a stepping stone toward future success. With supportive guidance, she can cultivate a mindset that sees possibility, embracing growth through every mistake and hiccup along the way. The role of family in nurturing this mindset cannot be overstated. A loving word from a parent, encouraging a child's persistence in the face of difficulty, can inspire great leaps of confidence and initiative.

Consider a boy, perhaps, who flounders during his first baseball game. As he stands at the plate, tension grips him. Striking out feels monumental—like the end of his dreams of becoming a star athlete. However, the words of a supportive coach or parent—gentle nudges of encouragement—can reframe this moment. Rather than viewing the moment solely as failure, he can come to understand it as a chance to build resilience. The CHOICE to pick up the bat again turns that strikeout into a lesson learned, reinforcing the notion that setbacks are mere stepping stones on the path to success.

It is through these formative experiences that CHOICES become pathways, interjecting themselves seamlessly into the lives of many children. Those who feel free to explore and express themselves tend to thrive, discovering their own passions through the act of learning. Each moment spent playing and exploring becomes a mosaic of experiences, where each memory adds color to the emergence of identity. Vivid images of a childhood spent believing in limitless possibilities persist long beyond the years of innocence.

Let us not forget, however, that each child's journey is inherently unique. One child may thrive on imagination, taking to the skies in their dreams, while another may find solace in the more grounded pleasures of constructing tangible things. Each path offers its own lessons, and the CHOICES made within these distinct experiences contribute to character development. The swirling chaos of childhood becomes a fertile ground, where dreams, aspirations, and limitations coexist in a delicate balance.

This balance can be seen vividly in the realm of creativity, where children express their boundless potential through art, music, and storytelling. The young girl who twirls in her dress becomes the artist—savvy with colors, creating worlds on a canvas where anything is possible. An abstract idea becomes a lifeline—her artwork becomes a voice for her thoughts, embodying dreams meticulously crafted. She learns to express herself, to break boundaries, and to convey her deepest yearnings.

In these moments, the reflections of parents take on a different form. They witness their children exploring life through art and imagination with pride. The CHOICE to nurture that creative expression opens doors to exploration of identity, teaching children that their voices matter and that their unique perspectives are valid. Here, they are encouraged to proceed boldly, to paint their narratives with authenticity. As a narrative unfolds through the power of creativity, the potential for limitless growth is anchored in the very fabric of their being.

Yet, it is crucial to recognize the significance of safeguarding this innocence to ensure the purity of potential remains intact. As the world imposes its structures and expectations, society often attempts to mold children within predefined boundaries. The belief that practicality trumps creativity can overshadow realms of infinite potential. How can we combat this encroachment on innocence while still celebrating the plethora of CHOICES available? Within these reflections, the answer lies in fostering an environment that allows exploration without fear, where parents and guardians become allies in the journey.

Cultivating spaces that encourage free thought and innovation allows children to blossom fully. Supportive interactions that celebrate exploration, encourage curiosity, and allow for mistakes are the backbone of instilling confidence in a child. When youth feel safe—and, more importantly, seen—they learn to navigate life's storms with resilience and resolve.

Consider the importance of family rituals—shared meals, story time under a comforting blanket, nature walks—that build authentic connections. In these moments, children experience the profound strength of togetherness, rooted in love and understanding. They begin to weave the threads of emotional intelligence, which shape their CHOICES and responses throughout their journeys.

As readers reflect on their own childhood narratives, they

may unearth the wisdom resting within their youthful experiences. How did familial bonds influence their paths? What dreams, once nurtured, were altered by the realities of growing up? Was there a moment of triumph where freedom over expectations catalyzed growth? By connecting with personal pasts, individuals can gain clarity on how those experiences shaped the very essence of their present decisions, igniting within them a desire for continued discovery.

Moreover, as individuals engage with the lessons learned from their youthful experiences, there also lies the potential for reversal or redefining of those early influences. Can one step back into that innocent realm of childhood? Can we embrace the aspirations birthed in that space where anything felt possible?

In the final stretch of this narrative, the call invites all to rekindle their own innate curiosity. To see life as an ever-evolving landscape of CHOICES requiring exploration and playfulness, inviting opportunity with each dawn. The essence of harnessing potential lies in forging connections—between the dreamer and the world, between the child within and the adult navigating life.

This journey acknowledges intrinsic themes of innocence

and potential, embracing the concept that in every child rests the heart of a creator. They carry with them the power to shape realities and seize futures steeped in possibilities. Whether brushing paint onto canvas or weaving stories through words, children teach us that dreams should never be dismissed. They show us that the dance with destiny begins with a single CHOICE, an invitation to take part in the grand adventure of life.

Thus, the subchapter draws to a gentle close yet invites readers to remain open-hearted and spirited as they continue to reflect on the intricate interplay of CHOICES and dreams that have shaped their journeys. Through the intoxicating lens of childhood, we are reminded that the essence of life dwells in the whispers of joy, in the hope waiting to unfurl like petals in the sun.

As we hold space for the dreamers of the world, let each adult embrace their past while encouraging the next generation to dream even bigger, to play bravely, and to dance freely across the broad canvas of existence. After all, in the dance of life, every CHOICE is but a step toward an infinite horizon of possibilities.

Growth Through CHOICES

In the tender years of childhood, every day presents a new opportunity for growth, shaped by the myriad CHOICES that define our early lives. Each CHOICE, no matter how seemingly insignificant, acts as a cornerstone in the foundation of our identity. From learning to walk to selecting our first friends, these small decisions create ripples that extend far beyond the immediate moment. They form the essence of who we are and guide us on our journey through the vast landscape of life.

Imagine a group of toddlers in a sunny park, each one teetering unsteadily on the cusp of walking. Some cling to the security of their parents' hands, while others take brave steps into the unknown, propelled by their burgeoning sense of independence. For many children, the decision to release their grip on the familiar and venture forth is a pivotal rite of passage. This single act of choosing to walk can symbolize a broader willingness to embrace change and take risks—a trait that will serve them well in the years to come.

As The Seeker begins to navigate the path of life, we witness how each decision influences their journey. The Seeker reflects on their first tentative steps, how the exhilaration of movement quickly gave way to the realization that walking also meant falling—often, and seemingly without warning. The scars of scraped knees serve as badges of honor, reminders of fights bravely fought against gravity and fear. Each struggle encountered along the way elevates their understanding of perseverance and resilience.

The Seeker recalls vivid memories of that early autumn morning, the leaves crunchy beneath tiny feet. They remember the joy of conquering wobbly steps and the delight in the encouraging cheers of friends and family. Yet, intertwined with these moments are the subtle yet profound CHOICES: Will they attempt to walk down the small hill or stay at their caregiver's side? Will they crawl back to safety or face the new environment with curiosity? Even these seemingly simple decisions forge a path toward independence, as confidence gradually blossoms.

As the childhood years unfold, the evolution of CHOICE deepens. A child's landscape is a playground of options, where every interaction can lead to new learning experiences. The Seeker finds themselves confronted by an array of fascinating possibilities: when to say "yes" or "no," whom to trust, and which friendships to cultivate. Each decision branches out, creating a vast web of relationships and experiences that fundamentally shape their worldview.

The friendships formed during these early years can significantly impact one's growth trajectory. The Seeker recalls their first real friend, a girl named Mia, who shared a similar passion for adventures. Together, they scrapped traditionally accepted boundaries, opting instead for exploration and imagination. Each invitation to play became a CHOICE that carved its mark into their developing identities. The laughter echoed in their minds, a permanent soundtrack of joy and acceptance, solidifying the belief that connection and partnership were integral parts of life.

However, not all CHOICES come as unblemished joys. As friendships blossom, they often present challenges as well. The Seeker faces their first true conflict—a misunderstanding with Mia that threatens to unravel their connection. Choosing whether to address the clash openly or bury it is a defining moment. In this instance, The Seeker opts for transparency, a decision born not just from love for their friend but also from a burgeoning awareness of the importance of communication in relationships. The healing that follows teaches them invaluable lessons about trust, regret, and ownership of one's part in conflict.

The CHOICE to cultivate relationships and confront difficulties is echoed in the CHOICES made by those surrounding The Seeker. Their parents' endeavors to instill values around respect, empathy, and self-expression become focal points of the growing environment. The Seeker learns observer lessons from familial interactions, noticing how love and difficult conversations can coexist. Each family dinner unfurls opportunities for connection, and they grow to appreciate the beauty of different perspectives through the stories shared around the table.

As childhood transitions into the murky waters of adolescence, decisions grow increasingly intricate. The playground evolves into a tapestry of social dynamics, presenting a complexity that often leaves one feeling overwhelmed. The Seeker grapples with the myriad CHOICES surrounding self-identity, peer pressure, and growing independence. This stage is a cauldron where the fear of exclusion collides with the desire for authenticity. It is in this tempest that The Seeker learns that the bravery involved in making CHOICES—whether to align with peers or stay true to oneself—forms the bedrock of their developing character.

During one memorable school project, The Seeker has a

chance to partner with a small group of peers. This scenario embodies the tension between artistic expression and adherence to group standards. Their peers lean toward a conservative, uninspired approach, while The Seeker yearns to introduce creativity and innovation. Here lies a crucial fork in their growth path: to conform for the sake of camaraderie or to risk vulnerability by advocating for their unique perspective.

In a moment of introspection, The Seeker chooses the latter. This decision catalyzes a pivotal shift not only in their own identity but also for the group. Their enthusiasm is infectious, awakening creativity in others, leading to a melding of thoughts and ideas. Through that project, The Seeker experiences the power of group collaboration, how individual CHOICES can lead to a richer outcome than any one person could achieve alone.

However, not every CHOICE bears applause. As The Seeker moves into high school, they increasingly confront the pervasive challenge of balancing personal desires with external expectations. The pressure to fit into social circles leads to a series of questionable decisions, resulting in conflict with their values. Each regret adds another thread to the tapestry of their journey, weaving lessons learned into the fabric of their identity. Through these CHOICES, they come to realize the importance of self-acceptance, evolving a deeper understanding of their authentic self.

It is amidst this growing complexity that The Seeker's experiences amplify their understanding of how small CHOICES build upon one another. Motivated by a desire for meaningful relationships and personal growth, they begin to make decisions that resonate with their emerging values. This transformation is not instant, but rather a gradual blossoming fueled by reflection and learning.

The Seeker looks back on a particular incident during their junior year—the CHOICE between attending a party with a new crowd and opting for a quiet evening alone to work on personal projects. The vibrant social scene pulsates enticingly, yet their intuition nudges them toward a different path. Choosing the solitary time paves the way for self-discovery. This intentional decision to prioritize understanding themselves over pleasing others marks a moment of maturation.

Through this act of CHOICE, transformative growth becomes evident. The Seeker discovers the joy of creative expression through writing, an avenue that allows them to articulate their thoughts and feelings with clarity. This decision becomes a cornerstone in rebuilding self-confidence and embracing vulnerability—the courage to put one's words out into the world without expectation of approval.

As the narrative unfolds, The Seeker observes how their early CHOICES influence others as well. Friends begin to take notice of their newfound spirit, leading to deeper connections rooted in authenticity. The CHOICES made in their teenage years radiate outward, encouraging others to partake in the journey of self-discovery and acceptance.

Life's decisions in the young adult phase can evoke uncertainty; yet, they also herald exciting adventures. The Seeker finds themselves faced with the prospect of attending college, a decision possessing both allure and trepidation. They ponder various pathways—ambitious dreams entwined with fear of the unknown. After moments of weighing possibilities, they choose a course of study aligned with their passions, a bravery underscored by reflective thought.

This CHOICE, seemingly colossal on the surface, brings about significant alteration in The Seeker's trajectory. It opens doors to internships and networking opportunities, expanding their worldview in ways they couldn't have fathomed. They recognize that every decision carries weight, weaving together the fabric of their emerging story.

In reflecting on their journey of CHOICES, The Seeker understands a crucial truth: growth is not linear; it ebbs and flows, each moment contributing to a broader arc of narrative. Key moments of decision shape their character dynamically, the interplay of joy and regret encircling their path.

More than once, The Seeker encounters setbacks—a difficult breakup, a challenging class, or feelings of isolation. Each instance embodies a lesson waiting to be learned. They acknowledge that CHOICES made during these challenging times can lead to profound insights about resilience and self-worth. By choosing to lean on supportive friendships or seek help during tough moments, The Seeker plants seeds of strength that flourish with time.

With every chapter closed, another opens, teaching The Seeker the immeasurable value of CHOICES made in the context of collaboration and mutual respect. They witness how every relationship holds transformative potential, influencing the fabric of individual and shared stories. Whether romantic, platonic, or familial, making conscious decisions continues to enrich their life, redefining what it means to grow through CHOICES.

In moments of deeper reflection, The Seeker invites readers to join in acknowledging their journeys. They ask us to recall key moments of CHOICE in our own lives—those moments where we chose courage over comfort, identity over acceptance. What CHOICES have shaped your identity? What small, seemingly insignificant CHOICES led to profound change? Reflecting on our histories allows us to authentically connect to the universal theme of growth through CHOICES.

In conclusion, every CHOICE propels us forward into the unknown. The journey through childhood, adolescence, and young adulthood expands upon the very essence of who we are, illustrating how each decision carves out the intricate masterpiece of existence. As we venture into new territories, may we carry the wisdom of our CHOICES and embrace the growth they yield.

Life, in all its uncertainty, offers a canvas upon which we paint our experiences—the brushstrokes alive with intention, meaning, and profound depth. The invitation to grow, prompted by conscious CHOICES, continues to beckon us as explorers on this remarkable journey called life.

Threads of Destiny

Weaving Our Tapestry

Life unfolds before us like an intricate tapestry, where the fabric of existence is woven from our myriad CHOICES. Each decision, whether grand or subtle, acts as a thread, contributing to the design of who we are and how we journey through the world. Just as a tapestry blends colors and textures, our lives are shaped by the CHOICES we make— CHOICES that resonate through time, crafting our destinies in ways often unseen.

Imagine the vibrant hues of red, blue, and gold in a tapestry, each thread meticulously stitched, representing moments of joy, love, and triumph. These bright colors embody our delightful experiences—the birth of new life, friendships forged, dreams realized. Yet, alongside these radiant threads, we weave darker strands—moments of loss, fear, and regret. Just as a beautiful tapestry requires light and shadow to create depth, our personal narratives gain richness by embracing both the luminous and somber threads of our stories.

In this reflective exploration, we accompany "The Mentor," a wise and nurturing figure who understands the interplay of light and dark in our life tapestries. The Mentor recognizes that both vibrant and shadowed threads are vital, fostering growth, resilience, and depth. Through their journey, we gain insight into how acknowledging the entirety of our experiences allows us to weave a more comprehensive narrative.

The Mentor's life exemplifies how CHOICES can enhance or detract from the beauty of our tapestries. One day, while teaching a group of eager students about the art of weaving, The Mentor shares their story, illuminating the essence of CHOICE in shaping the fabric of life.

"Each of you holds a thread in your hand," The Mentor begins, gesturing toward the colored strands before the students. "These threads symbolize your CHOICES. Just as you select colors to weave into your tapestry, you choose how to respond to life's events. Every decision creates a unique pattern on the loom of your existence. But remember, not all threads need to be vibrant."

The students, intrigued, listen intently as The Mentor explains that vibrant threads represent joyous, momentous decisions, while darker threads symbolize life's inevitable challenges. Life, The Mentor clarifies, is not merely a collection of joyful moments but a complex array of experiences that, together, create a meaningful existence.

Reflecting on their past, The Mentor recalls a childhood moment. "I remember when my father taught me to weave. He handed me my first thread—a bright, sunny yellow. That day, I was filled with optimism, eager to create. As I wove that yellow into my tapestry, I laughed, imagining a wonderful future. But life had other plans. Soon, the blue of disappointment and the gray of uncertainty crept in."

The Mentor pauses, letting their words resonate. "I realized not all my threads would be luminous. There were moments when I chose the comfort of familiarity—a dull, gray thread that stifled creativity. But there were also times when I braved the unknown, weaving in bright greens and purples of growth and exploration."

The students begin to consider their own tapestries—the colors and textures shaped by their decisions. Reflective questions arise:

- What CHOICES have shaped the vibrant parts of my tapestry?

- What darker threads are woven within, and how do they influence my design?

- How can I weave in new colors to enrich my life's fabric?

Life's tapestry is also about community—the shared experiences that connect us, creating interwoven fabrics of connection. The Mentor explains how our CHOICES affect not only our own tapestries but also those of others.

"When I committed to my education wholeheartedly, it transformed my path. That CHOICE not only brightened my tapestry but also inspired my friends and family to pursue their own educational journeys. Our lives began to intertwine, each decision enriching the collective fabric we share."

Touched by this realization, the students appreciate the interconnectedness of their lives. They see the beauty in how threads merge, creating a broader narrative that reflects both individual and shared journeys.

As the conversation deepens, The Mentor introduces the complexity of regret—the unmade CHOICES that haunt our tapestries. The pain of hindsight can cast a shadow over the vibrant colors we strive to weave. The Mentor shares a solemn memory of a moment when a CHOICE was deferred.

"Once, I hesitated to speak my truth to a dear friend, letting fear silence me. That CHOICE weighed heavily, an invisible thread of regret woven into my fabric. Each time I replayed that moment, I saw its imprint—dull, gray, and heavy, overshadowing the vibrant threads around it. It wasn't until I accepted that moment as part of my tapestry—and the learning it brought—that I could fully embrace the brilliance of my present."

The students nod, understanding the importance of embracing every aspect of their stories. Reflecting on their experiences, they see how regrets can serve as catalysts for growth rather than anchors holding them back.

The Mentor emphasizes the ripple effect of CHOICES.

"Consider how each vibrant thread you add not only enriches your story but also elevates the stories of others. When I choose kindness, that thread vibrates outward, influencing my children, friends, and community—each growing thread linking us to a tapestry far broader than ourselves."

The students ponder the responsibility of their CHOICES. Their tapestries aren't just for themselves; they're for everyone touched by their decisions.

The Mentor encourages the students to craft their tapestries intentionally. "Take note of the colors and textures in your life. Are there threads you wish to weave more of? What patterns are emerging, and how do they make you feel?"

In silence, the students envision their tapestries, considering the moments that have shaped their designs: the vibrant colors of childhood laughter, the subtle pastels of first loves, the sharp blacks of loss, and the rich golds of resilience and achievement—all woven into a unique story.

To guide this self-exploration, The Mentor offers reflective questions:

- What are the most vibrant colors in my tapestry?
- What dark threads are woven in, and how have they shaped my experience?

- What patterns emerge in my CHOICES?

- How can I weave in new colors that reflect the person I aspire to be?

The atmosphere grows contemplative as students share their reflections—stories of colorful CHOICES and challenging moments. Laughter and tears intermingle, highlighting the beauty of vulnerability and connection in acknowledging the full spectrum of their experiences.

An energetic current passes through the room as a shared understanding unfolds. Each person's tapestry is both an individual masterpiece and part of a collective narrative. The students laugh, cry, and grow together, stitching a rich tapestry of shared experiences, illuminated by the CHOICES they make.

As the chapter closes, The Mentor imparts final wisdom: "Every CHOICE can add new colors to your tapestry. Approach each decision with intention, reflecting on the legacy you wish to leave and how those colors inspire others. Embrace life's vibrancy and complexity, including its tangles. Each twist is part of your unique pattern, reflecting not only who you are but also the influence you have on the world. Your tapestry is your legacy, evolving with each CHOICE."

The students leave with renewed purpose, ready to weave beautifully complex tapestries filled with color, depth, texture, and emotion—truly embracing the art of life's journey.

Facing the Shadows

In the intricate tapestry of our lives, vibrant colors of joy and success intertwine with darker threads of regret and failure. These shadows can loom large, often overshadowing the brighter hues. Each CHOICE, every path taken, can leave a thread of uncertainty, a whisper of doubt echoing long after decisions are made. This subchapter explores the honest yet challenging journey of facing these shadows, inviting introspection on the CHOICES that haunt us and illuminating how to transform them into beacons of learning.

Life is not a straight path. It twists and turns, presenting crossroads where CHOICE is both a privilege and a necessity. The "Doubter," a character embodying our internal fears and insecurities, faces these crossroads with a heavy heart. Each significant decision brings the specter of past failures, casting doubt on their ability to choose wisely. This lingering sense of impending missteps can paralyze or deter us from pursuing the life we desire.

With each failure, a shadow of regret emerges. Questions

like "What if I had chosen differently?" or "Could I have avoided this pain?" embody the fabric of self-doubt, creating a grip that can hinder progress. Yet, facing these shadows is not a sign of weakness but a testament to courage. Confronting our deepest fears and unraveling the threads of despair allows us to weave a new story of hope and resilience.

Creativity, such as art or journaling, offers profound opportunities for catharsis. It serves as a mirror, reflecting the complexity of our experiences. Journaling, in particular, provides a sacred space for thoughts to flow freely, undisturbed by judgment. By writing about our fears, regrets, and failures, we make them tangible, freeing ourselves from their emotional hold. This process allows us to explore darker moments with an unflinching gaze, recognizing vulnerability as a powerful ally.

One exercise involves reflecting on a specific regretful CHOICE. Write about the event, detailing not only what happened but how it made you feel. What thoughts plagued you? Did fear hold you back from a decision that felt right? Allow emotions—anger, sadness, clarity, doubt—to flow. The goal is to unpack the experience and understand the recurring feelings it evokes, revealing the footprints these shadows leave behind.

Visual art can add another layer of exploration. Create a piece that represents both regret and emergence from it. Use colors, forms, and symbols that resonate with your emotions. This visual expression can be transformative, embracing the chaotic beauty of failure and pain.

Confronting these emotions forges pathways toward acceptance. The Doubter learns that shadows hold valuable lessons, serving as narrative guides rather than life sentences. Regret does not define us; it refines us. Each dark thread vies to teach us how to navigate future CHOICES with greater wisdom.

Consider that your shadows hold lessons. A seemingly trivial CHOICE may have taught you to weigh decisions carefully. A misstep may have revealed unforeseen strengths. Allow yourself to recognize the bittersweet beauty of these experiences and their role in shaping your present self.

Confronting regret prompts vital questions: Are our fears rooted in transformative moments or mere perceptions? Can we choose narratives that empower rather than disempower? Here, accountability emerges—life is not just about recognizing shadows but choosing how to respond to them.

Redefine the narratives attached to your shadows. Instead

of viewing failure as evidence of incompetence, see it as a stepping stone toward growth. Through this lens, regret can transform into gratitude for lessons learned, fostering a journey of self-discovery where imperfections are acknowledged but do not hinder self-love.

Sharing these experiences with others can uncover surprising connections. Building a community where shadows are openly discussed mitigates the isolation of regret. These shared struggles highlight our common humanity, stripping the Doubter of their singular nature. In vulnerable spaces, we realize we are not alone; we are bonded by our experiences and CHOICES.

As you navigate your shadows, honor your story. Those darker threads serve a purpose within your tapestry. Reflect on what they represent and how they inspire empathy, responsibility, and understanding. Let them push you toward resilience, teaching you the power of CHOICE and the beauty of living intentionally.

To engage with your shadows, create intentional moments for exploration. Establish an art ritual—choose a space, gather materials, and allow time for creative expression. Evoke emotions tied to past regrets while channeling them into visual stories. This practice can lead to emotional release, illuminating pathways for healing.

Alternatively, try shadow work, a psychological practice delving into the darker aspects of identity. Write letters to your shadows, addressing the CHOICES that haunt you. Invite them to speak, uncovering motivations and fears beneath the surface. Express gratitude for their lessons while asserting your intent to move forward.

Through this work, acceptance deepens. The Doubter learns that shadows do not negate brightness but signify a life fully lived, marked by humanity's imperfections. These threads weave into a larger design of resilience, instilling confidence to rise above fears and shape your reality.

In conclusion, shadows are integral to the human experience, reminding us that life is an intricate tapestry of CHOICES and consequences. Every decision, regardless of outcome, contributes to our journey, illuminating the path toward growth and wisdom. Acknowledge these darker threads; embrace them as part of your narrative. By doing so, you empower yourself to rewrite regret as a chapter of possibility and transformation.

Commit to ongoing reflection through journaling, artistic

expression, or community sharing. Lean into your shadows—they hold lessons waiting to be uncovered. As you weave these threads into your tapestry, remember that you hold the power to redefine your narrative, shaping a vivid and colorful existence that honors both the light and dark within you.

Discovering the Unseen Threads

Life is a tapestry woven from the threads of our CHOICES—some bold and vibrant, others subtle and muted. As we journey through existence, we often overlook the quieter decisions that shape our paths. CHOICES that seem insignificant at first glance can, upon closer examination, reveal themselves to be monumental. In this subchapter, we unravel the unseen threads that weave through the fabric of our lives, exploring how minor decisions can lead to profound transformations.

Imagine a tranquil moment in a bustling coffee shop. A young woman named Lily sits quietly in a corner, her fingers wrapped around a steaming cup of chai tea. As she observes the crowd around her, she is lost in thought. Unbeknownst to her, a simple CHOICE—to sit at this particular table rather than another—will alter the course of her life.

Earlier that morning, Lily faced a decision: wake up early to work on her latest painting or sleep in and rush through her day. After much internal debate, she chose the latter, believing she could paint later. This decision led her to the coffee shop for a quick dose of caffeine before work. By choosing this specific table, her world turned upside down.

At the neighboring table sat Mark, a gallery owner, flipping through portfolios of potential artists. Lily's decision to sit where she did allowed her to overhear snippets of Mark's conversation. Intrigued, she gathered her courage and struck up a conversation. That seemingly inconsequential CHOICE became an opportunity to present her work, launching her artistic career. What began as a simple decision transformed into the launchpad for her dreams.

This vignette highlights the importance of noticing the quiet CHOICES we make daily. Each decision, no matter how small, is a thread in the tapestry of our lives. As we navigate the mundane moments of existence, we often miss their significance. Time itself is composed of countless CHOICES, each holding transformative potential.

Consider Sarah, a finance professional, who wandered into a used bookstore one evening after work. Meandering through the narrow aisles, her fingers trailed along the spines of books. Selecting a novel by a lesser-known author, she hardly anticipated its impact. Inspired by the story, Sarah explored her own writing, embarking on a side career as a novelist. This shift enriched her life with creativity and offered a new means of self-expression.

Subtle decisions accumulate, creating a ripple effect that guides us down various paths. These paths affect not only our journeys but also those of others connected to us. A simple hello or act of kindness can set off an unlikely chain reaction. Consider James, a man at a crossroads. Faced with a long commute and a stressful job, he often stopped at a local park for lunch. One day, he chose to walk a different route, seeking a change of scenery. This small deviation led him to meet a stranger who became a close friend, introducing him to a volunteer organization that reshaped his life's priorities.

What began as a lunch break evolved into regular volunteering, filling James with purpose and joy. The CHOICE to walk a different route became a thread that led to a community of like-minded individuals celebrating kindness and service. As he sat in a circle of friends sharing heartfelt stories each week, James realized how one simple decision could open a doorway to a new reality.

Our lives are filled with such CHOICES, yet we often

overlook their significance. Cultivating mindfulness in our daily decisions, even the trivial ones, allows us to appreciate their transformative potential. By recognizing the beauty of these unseen threads, we become active participants in our life narratives.

The notion of CHOICE extends beyond life-altering decisions like pursuing a new career or relocating. It lies in everyday moments—what to say to a friend, how to respond to a stranger, or even what to wear. Each CHOICE is interwoven with our desires, fears, and values. These seemingly minor decisions shape not only our lives but also the world around us.

The interconnections of our CHOICES form a fragile yet resilient web. Like threads in a tapestry, they are intricately linked. The gentlest CHOICE can lead to astounding outcomes if nurtured over time.

Consider the CHOICES within our relationships. The friendships we foster hinge on small decisions—whom we reach out to, the energy we bring to conversations, and how present we are. Reflect on Lily and Mark: had Lily not engaged, she would have missed a chance to connect deeply.

Another compelling story is Mia's, a graphic designer

feeling creatively stuck. One evening, she chose to attend a local art meetup instead of staying home to binge-watch television. That reluctant decision opened her to discussions with artists and designers who inspired her to take creative risks. Soon, Mia embarked on a path of self-discovery, moving beyond her routine and reigniting her passion through personal projects.

Every CHOICE has the power to shift our life's trajectory. The unseen threads remind us to act with intentionality, infusing awareness into our daily decisions. By paying attention to these threads, we unlock the potential to shape our paths and enrich our lives.

We must also embrace the responsibility of our CHOICES. Each decision reverberates through the lives of others, creating a web of interconnectedness that illustrates the fabric of community. A single CHOICE can transform others in ways we may not foresee.

The decision-making process is layered with complexity; what seems inconsequential to us may hold immense significance for another. As we navigate the CHOICES that define our lives, cultivating empathy and awareness allows us to weave kindness and compassion into our decisions, recognizing that every thread holds purpose.

The unseen threads also invite reflection on our patterns of CHOICE. Examining the decisions we make consistently reveals the narratives shaping our lives. Sarah, for instance, discovered that her tendency to please others drove many of her CHOICES. By recognizing this pattern, she began making deliberate decisions aligned with her authentic self rather than external expectations.

Recognizing these threads deepens our self-awareness, encouraging us to reflect on the intentions behind our CHOICES. By evaluating their interconnectedness, we empower ourselves to refine our paths intentionally.

Small deviations can lead to new vistas, broadening our experiences. The freedom to weave new threads into our tapestry invites exploration. As we reflect on these unseen threads, gratitude enhances our perspective. Acknowledging the CHOICES of others deepens our appreciation for the relationships that brighten our world. Had James hesitated to reach out to his new friend, he might have missed a transformative shift in his life.

Incorporating gratitude into our CHOICES fosters interconnectedness and invites us to celebrate the threads woven by friendships, mentorships, and acts of kindness. Our tapestry becomes more vibrant when we honor these connections.

As we conclude this exploration of the unseen threads, remember that every decision is an opportunity—a chance to shape a narrative filled with creativity, empathy, and growth. Cultivate awareness and presence in your CHOICES, unlocking the potential hidden in life's mundane moments.

Encourage yourself and others to engage with the delicate threads that connect us. Each decision invites new possibilities and adventures. Just as Lily's CHOICE to sit at a different table led to new opportunities, your CHOICES can alter your life's course and resonate for generations.

As you move forward, reflect daily on the unseen threads of your CHOICES. Embrace the joy of recognizing how decisions, both large and small, weave the fabric of your unique journey. Lean into your power as an active participant in your life's narrative, weaving it with love, intention, and purpose.

Consider the quiet decisions awaiting you. What small yet significant CHOICES demand your attention? How can you honor the unseen threads connecting you to others? Each day offers countless opportunities to explore and affirm your narrative, ensuring your life's tapestry is rich with purpose and meaning.

The Fork in the Road

Pivotal Moments

In every life, there come moments that alter our trajectories—crucial decisions that feel much like standing at a fork in the road. These pivotal moments have the power to shape our destiny, and as we navigate them, we often find ourselves challenged to embrace uncertainty, take a leap of faith, or stay within our perceived safety zones. It is in these encounters—whether in career CHOICES, relationships, or relocating to an entirely new place—that we discover the essence of who we are meant to become.

Consider the first time you faced a significant career decision. Perhaps you graduated from school, cap and gown adorning your excitement and hope for the future. The world lay open before you, a vast landscape of possibilities. Yet, lurking beneath that thrill resided a knot of anxiety. Do I follow my passion or choose the safe path? Friends around you seemed equally perplexed. Some would take the plunge into entrepreneurial ventures, driven by dreams of starting something revolutionary. Others would opt for stability in corporate roles, aiming for a secure salary and benefits. You stood at a point of divergence, a metaphorical fork in the road, where each CHOICE had its own implications.

Reflecting on this shared experience stirs memories of excitement and dread. Your heart danced at the thought of pursuing your passion, while your mind conjured images of financial instability and uncertainty. Emotions intertwined in a dizzying ballet, urging you to seize this moment and sculpt your future. Ultimately, you chose your path, whether it was to forge ahead in your dream career or opt for a more traditional route, leaving an indelible mark on your journey.

In the realm of relationships, the impact of pivotal

moments often surfaces in life's most profound experiences. Think back to your first love, that exhilarating rush of emotions, the sparks ignited in youthful bliss. Yet, as with all relationships, a defining point emerged where you had to decide whether to commit or walk away. Maybe it was a conversation about your future, a trivial squabble unveiling deeper incompatibilities, or the first whisper of doubts. You found yourself at another fork, grappling with the emotional weight of your decision. Would you lean into vulnerability, embarking on a journey of shared dreams and possible heartache, or safeguard your heart by retreating into solitude?

This moment was laden with the significance of learning and growth. For many, the stakes were as high as they could be, influencing emotional well-being for years to come. Choosing to commit could lead to the joy of shared laughter and discovery, whereas opting out could yield self-discovery and newfound independence. Despite the outcome, what was essential was the courage it took to confront that fork and make a CHOICE, guiding your heart in the direction it longed to go.

Reflect upon relocation as the next pivotal CHOICE, one that all too often invites inner conflict. Perhaps a job opportunity beckoned from another city, promising advancement and a chance to spread your wings. At the same time, it demanded an uprooting—a leaving behind of familiar places, friends, and the comfort of the known. The allure of an exciting new chapter was enticing, yet tinged with trepidation. Could you find a community as warm and welcoming as the one you'd left? Would loneliness loom larger than adventure?

In moments like these, you stand amidst a swirl of possibilities. Would you follow your ambition, ready to pivot toward growth, or would you hesitate, tethered by fear? Making the decision required patience and deep reflection, often calling upon your strongest convictions. What followed was a leap into the unknown, driven by the hope of a fulfilling career or the belief that change could flourish into something beautiful.

To represent these universal experiences more vividly, let's explore a few relatable anecdotes that illuminate the essence of pivotal moments.

In her heart, Claire held dreams of being a graphic designer, fueled by an unquenchable passion for creativity. After completing her degree, she was presented with two job offers: one from a well-established agency offering steady pay and benefits, a secure environment; the other, a startup bursting with potential but fraught with risk. Each CHOICE weighed heavily on her. Feeling trapped at her own fork, she sought counsel from mentors, friends, and family.

One evening, sitting cross-legged in her living room, she visualized the offer letters on the coffee table, staring at them as if they were portals into her future. The steady income from the agency lured her with assurances of stability, while the vibrancy of the startup ignited her passion. After sleepless nights filled with doubts and indecision, she took a deep breath and chose the startup, stepping beyond her comfort zone. The exhilarating rush of creativity ignited her spirit, and despite the struggles early on, she never looked back. The journey was fraught with challenges, but Claire had chosen growth.

Another story brings us to Michael, who faced a fork at the crossroads of relationships. Recently divorced and carrying the weight of heartache, he found himself amidst a burgeoning connection with Sara, a spirited woman filled with wonder and warmth. Yet, shadows loomed as he wrestled with vulnerability. Would he let someone in again, risking further hurt? After much introspection, he recognized that the yearning for companionship was greater than his fear of being hurt again.

On the eve of their anniversary, Michael made the conscious decision to lay bare his insecurities, crafting their bond on honesty rather than uncertainty. Their relationship deepened that night, and Sara held him close, erasing the solitude that had once engulfed him. By embracing the uncertainties born from his past, he forged something beautiful and lasting—an affirmation of love emerging from life's heavy lessons.

As we turn the lens toward relocation, consider the experience of Alex, a young professional who received an unexpected job offer in a city thousands of miles away. The thought of leaving his hometown—the birthplace of cherished memories—felt akin to shedding a part of himself. Friends and family peppered him with mixed messages: some applauded the adventure and opportunity for growth, while others watched in disbelief as he contemplated leaving.

On a rainy afternoon, Alex stood at the junction of excitement and fear, envisioning his future among the city skyscrapers. With a leap of faith, he decided to accept the position, ready to say goodbye to the familiar streets of his childhood. The first few weeks were overwhelming—

navigating a new workplace, learning the public transport system, and facing the daunting solitude of an empty apartment. But with time, the vibrant energy of the city enveloped him, and he forged new connections, finding joy in every corner of his new existence.

These stories underscore the essence of pivotal moments: they challenge us to reflect and decide. It is in that reflection we uncover the courage to take risks and embrace the unknown. Consider how your own experiences mirror these tales—think about the forks you've encountered and the CHOICES you made.

Let us pause here for a moment and invite you to visualize your own forks in the road. Picture yourself standing before two distinct paths, unsure of where each might lead. Bring to mind the emotional responses associated with those moments: Were you anxious, excited, afraid, or hopeful? How did fear or excitement sway your decision? Each of these emotions is a guiding star, leading you toward growth, often illuminating alternatives you may not have previously considered.

Encourage yourself to write down these pivotal moments, those slices of life shaped by your CHOICES. What decisions have stirred profound emotions? What thoughts surfaced each time you reached a fork? Ponder the significance and the resulting growth from those experiences. Remember, contemplation opens the door to a deeper understanding of oneself.

Pivotal moments should be viewed not as daunting dilemmas, but rather as opportunities for growth that beckon us toward the unknown. Embrace the uncertainty, for it is in navigating these paths that we develop our voices, our stories, and our destinies.

As you begin to reflect on these decisions, ask yourself: How did each experience empower you to step closer to your true self? What lessons did you learn from each fork? These inquiries hold valuable insights into your journey and are essential for nurturing growth along the winding roads of life.

When we step back and embrace a broader perspective of pivotal moments, we realize that each CHOICE we make is part of a greater narrative, perhaps even a symphonic orchestra of experiences that color the journey of our lives. Each fork opens a new measure, a new melody, in our ongoing composition. Finding courage to explore these CHOICES helps us craft richer tapestries woven with the experiences we've encountered along the way.

As we near the conclusion of this exploration, it is paramount to consider how pivotal moments imprint not just our lives but extend beyond ourselves into the world around us. Every CHOICE leads to consequences; hence, our decisions inevitably shape the experiences of others—loved ones, friends, and even acquaintances can be influenced by the paths we choose.

Imagine sharing your story with a younger generation, potentially lighting a spark in them as they navigate their own forks. Each decision becomes a part of their tapestry, reminding them that courage can turn uncertainties into opportunities. This realization underscores the moral responsibility we hold as we travel through life, embracing and celebrating the forks we encounter.

Ultimately, life offers a myriad of paths, each representing a unique story of growth. We are given opportunities to choose, time and again, and with each CHOICE, we carve our destiny in the universe. So, as we navigate the forks and pivotal moments in our lives, let us strive to embrace the unknown, find meaning, and foster courage in our hearts.

Stand tall at the forks in the road you encounter, for each

one is an invitation to grow, evolve, and embark on a journey that leads you to your truest self. Celebrate the fears, the uncertainties, and the exhilarating joy of taking leaps. Each moment calls you to step forward fearlessly, armed with the wealth of experiences that have shaped you—a beautiful tapestry of the CHOICES you've made.

Embracing Possibility

In a quiet moment, when the world around you is hushed, pause to consider the crossroads of your life. Each fork in the road beckons with promises of adventure, uncertainty, and a blend of beauty and terror. You stand at these thresholds, aware that the CHOICES you make will carve pathways not only for you but also for those around you. Introduced through the lens of "The Dreamer," we will embark on a journey that illuminates the possibilities of these intersections, celebrating the marvelous complexity of our decision-making process.

Our protagonist, The Dreamer, often found themselves daydreaming about the future. The vibrant colors of their aspirations painted a picture of life that was both enticing and overwhelming. Who would they become? Which paths would they take? As The Dreamer sat under their favorite oak tree, the vastness of the CHOICES before them felt both exhilarating and daunting.

The beauty of CHOICES lies in their inherent potential. Each decision sprouts from a moment of possibility, with its roots anchored deep within our values, experiences, and the dreams we nurture. Yet, at the same time, this wealth of options can manifest as a paralyzing fear. As The Dreamer gazed into the distance, contemplating a leap into the unknown, they could feel a familiar tug of anxiety.

What if they made the wrong CHOICE? The thought loomed large in their mind, casting shadows on the vibrant scenes of success they had envisioned. Yet, upon deeper reflection, The Dreamer acknowledged that the fear of making a wrong CHOICE was a part of the journey. To grow, one must learn to navigate these fears with courage and an open heart.

To illustrate the tide of emotions at these crossroads, let's journey alongside The Dreamer in a moment that changed their life forever. In their college years, The Dreamer found themselves enthralled by two passions: art and psychology. On one hand, an artist's canvas would allow them to express feelings as vivid as a summer sunset. On the other, the intimacy of understanding human behavior drew them into the psychological realm, promising the chance to delve into the intricacies of the mind.

One fateful evening, a special opportunity arose. An internship program combined both fields, offering a part-time position at a community center where they could create art therapy workshops. It seemed to be the perfect blend of The Dreamer's passions. However, this precious opportunity came at a cost: it required relocating to a new city that felt both exhilarating and terrifying.

In the days leading up to their decision, The Dreamer oscillated between hope and fear. Would they thrive? What if the move disrupted their comfort and security? The familiar beckoned, while the allure of the unknown whispered tantalizing promises of growth and fulfillment.

In that pivotal moment, The Dreamer realized that embracing possibility meant accepting risk. They made a bold CHOICE, packing their bags and leaving the security of their hometown behind. Within weeks, they found themselves in a new city, stepping into a reality that shimmered with potential.

The story doesn't end there. Immediately, The Dreamer encountered challenges—adjusting to a new environment, meeting new people, and facing the inevitable ups and downs of life. But with every step, they discovered something fundamental: possibility flourishes when coupled with courage.

One afternoon, as The Dreamer facilitated their first art therapy session, the fear that once held them back dissipated, replaced by a warmth that coursed through their being. They watched as participants opened up, sharing stories and emotions they had long kept hidden. It was in this space of vulnerability, where creation met healing, that The Dreamer recognized the power of making CHOICES rooted in passion.

Life, much like art, is about embracing all colors—even those that seem dark or daunting at first. Each brushstroke carries the weight of decisions made, interwoven with the story that ultimately unfolds. The Dreamer, now thriving in their new role, learned to view each CHOICE as an opportunity to add depth to their personal canvas.

Now, consider your own life's forks. Where are you standing at an intersection? Which passions light a fire in your spirit? Take a moment to reflect on the possibilities that lie before you, and ask yourself the following questions:

- What are the options available to me right now?

- Which CHOICE excites me, even if it feels intimidating?

- How can embracing risk in my CHOICES lead to personal growth?

As you ponder these inquiries, let's transition to a creative exercise that can help you unpack your own possibilities:

1. **Visualize Your Crossroads**: Draw a simple diagram that represents your current life situation. Label the major paths (CHOICES) before you. Use colors, words, or symbols to translate your feelings about each option.

2. **Storyboarding Your Future**: Select one option you feel compelled to pursue. Create a storyboard that maps out the potential journey. What are the initial steps? What challenges might arise? How will you overcome them? Fill the storyboard with sketches, words, and images that inspire you.

3. **The Risks and Rewards List**: Make a two-column list. On one side, write down the potential risks of pursuing this path. On the other, detail the

rewards and benefits you hope to gain.

As you engage in these exercises, channel The Dreamer's spirit. Embrace the possibilities as they open before you with each mindful stroke of your pen or brush. Remember that each CHOICE has the power to propel you into new and exhilarating territories.

While some roads may lead to unexpected challenges, every step into the unknown offers lessons that contribute to your journey. As The Dreamer continued to navigate their chosen path, they understood that challenges would emerge, yet each moment would become a brushstroke in the larger painting of their life—an ever-evolving masterpiece.

Life's intersections, while saturated with uncertainty, can also illuminate the path to profound revelations. Think back to The Dreamer's experience at the community center; they did not merely strive to overcome obstacles but transformed them into stepping stones toward personal empowerment. Through vulnerability, they connected with others and learned to trust the flow of life.

It's significant to highlight that embracing possibilities requires relinquishing the need for perfection. Perfection can become a cage that stifles creativity and deters risk-taking.

Instead, seek authenticity—what feels true to you?

Collect stories and experiences of others who dared to leap into the void of uncertainty. Perhaps there's a friend who transitioned careers, a mentor who paved their path in unexpected ways, or a historical figure who changed the world through their CHOICES. Each narrative carries a gem of wisdom that enriches the understanding of embracing possibility.

These stories resonate with The Dreamer's journey. They illustrate that while life may present fear, it also provides opportunities for joy, connection, and growth. Embrace every facet of your experience—both beauty and imperfection—as you continue your expedition.

Life is an intricate tapestry woven from threads of decisions. The colors may shift as CHOICES intersect, but it's essential to remain open to the broader spectrum. Are you leaning into joy despite the fear? Are you allowing love to surge forth amid uncertainty? This process may require rewriting your story periodically as new opportunities arise.

At this point, let's step back into a reflective space. Pause to consider the entirety of your CHOICES and their implications. What stories do they tell about who you are?

How will the CHOICES you make today echo into your future?

As you observe this ripple effect, consider implementing a personal mantra. Perhaps it might be: "I embrace possibility and trust the journey ahead." Repeating this affirmation allows for a cultural shift within yourself, grounding you in the belief that every CHOICE matters, and every path leads to valuable experiences.

To further deepen your journey of embracing possibility, engage in these closing exercises:

1. **Dream Your Potential**: Write a letter to your future self. Enthusiastically describe the adventures you hope to embark on, the CHOICES you plan to make, and the person you long to become.

2. **Future Vision Board**: Using visuals from magazines or online sources, create a vision board that embodies the possibilities you adore. This tactile representation will serve as a reflection of your dreams and a reminder of the roads you may choose to pursue.

3. **Gratitude Mapping**: Craft a map of gratitude reflecting the CHOICES that have already shaped your life positively. Identify what you have gained

from each important CHOICE you've made and how it has led you to this crossroads.

Embracing possibility is a conscious CHOICE. It requires a balance of faith in oneself and a willingness to step into the unknown. The power rests within you to create a mesmerizing narrative from the crossroads you encounter.

In closing, as The Dreamer embarked on their journey, they learned to embrace faith in their CHOICES, knowing that each decision was an invitation to construct a life filled with purpose and passion. The beauty of possibility lies not only in the destination but in the richness of each moment along the way. May you find the courage to embrace the infinite possibilities that await you at every fork in your road.

Navigating Setbacks

As we stand at the crossroads of life, the elements of CHOICE loom large, and yet, often clouded within those CHOICES lies the inevitability of setbacks. These can emerge as shadows from poor decisions, whispering reminders of our fallibility. In this section, we will explore these setbacks—those frustrating detours that beckon us to reconsider the paths we've taken—and how they can transform our understanding of life's journey.

The "Doubter" character embodies the insecurities and fears that often accompany setbacks. Many of us have felt a twinge of doubt creeping in after a decision that led to unexpected consequences. Perhaps it was the job CHOICE that didn't quite fit, the relationship that soured, or the impulsive investment that failed to yield returns. The "Doubter" speaks to us all, presenting the very real emotions tied to our experiences.

Setbacks do not merely signify loss; they offer a unique opportunity for growth and reflection. The notion of seeing setbacks as valuable lessons, rather than just impediments on our journey, is a critical shift in mindset. It beckons us to dig deeper into the fabric of our experiences—to confront and, more importantly, to rationalize the anxieties that may follow.

To navigate through these cloudy waters of doubt, we can engage in guided reflections that allow us to evaluate the paths we've taken. These reflections will not only serve to highlight mistakes but also to extract the invaluable lessons learned through navigating these turbulent waters.

Understanding the Nature of Setbacks

Let's begin by defining what a setback truly is in the context of our CHOICES. A setback is often perceived as an obstacle that hinders progress, a moment that disrupts the flow of our journey. The "Doubter" might remind us of the discomfort associated with setbacks—a sense of failure, inadequacy, or lost opportunities. But if we dig deeper, we can uncover the multifaceted nature of setbacks.

1. **Obstacles as Teachers:** Setbacks can serve as important teachers, revealing areas of ourselves that need strengthening. For instance, consider an individual who chooses a career path driven solely by external validation, perhaps the allure of prestige rather than genuine interest. If that CHOICE leads to dissatisfaction or burnout, the subsequent setback doesn't merely represent a failure but a lesson in understanding one's true passions and desires. This internal learning can steer future decisions toward more fulfilling CHOICES.

2. **Emotional Responses:** Emotions play a significant role in how we perceive setbacks. The "Doubter" often brings forth feelings such as regret, fear, and anxiety. A failed business venture, for example, can trigger intense emotional responses ranging from embarrassment to self-blame. It's crucial to acknowledge these feelings, as they are part of the

human experience. By confronting these emotions, we can begin to rationalize them, understand their roots, and ultimately free ourselves from their grip.

3. **The Reflection Process:** Evaluating past decisions allows us to step back and analyze what went wrong. This evaluation can generate clarity that helps refine our decision-making process moving forward. Consider using reflective journals, engaging in conversations with trusted friends, or working with mentors to dissect setbacks constructively. These practices can shed light on blind spots, helping to cultivate wisdom from experience.

Confronting the Voice of Doubt

As we venture into the landscape of setbacks, the "Doubter" becomes more pronounced. This character personifies the fears that manifest after a poor decision has led to challenges. Understanding this voice can empower us to confront it with rational perspectives.

1. **Identifying Patterns:** The first step is to listen to the voice of the "Doubter" and identify the patterns that frequently emerge in our self-dialogue. What are the phrases or experiences that trigger

feelings of inadequacy? It might be thoughts like, "I should have known better" or "I failed, and now my future is compromised." Acknowledging these patterns allows us to separate our identity from our mistakes.

2. **Reframing Setbacks:** The next step is to reframe how we view setbacks. Instead of labeling ourselves as failures, we can state that we made CHOICES based on the best information available at the time. The language we use can influence our emotions. For instance, saying, "This situation teaches me a valuable lesson" can foster resilience. It illustrates that setbacks are not the end but rather opportunities for learning and transformation.

3. **Affirmations and Self Compassion:** Employ affirmations as a tool to combat the negative narrative from the "Doubter." Simple affirmations, such as "I am capable of learning from my experiences" or "Setbacks do not define my worth," create a positive reference point. Self-compassion is also critical in this process. Treat yourself with the same kindness you would offer a friend; recognize that making mistakes is part of being human.

Taking Action: Practical Steps to Overcome Setbacks

With the insights gained from understanding setbacks and confronting doubts, we can embark on actionable steps to move beyond past decisions. While the path forward will vary from person to person, certain principles can guide the way.

1. **Analyze:** Begin by analyzing the situation. Break down the specifics of the setback: what led you here? Reflect on the decisions made that resulted in this outcome. Question the assumptions that underpinned those CHOICES. This analytical view can foster a deeper understanding and present clues for future decision-making.

2. **Identify and Accept Emotions:** Allow yourself to feel and acknowledge the emotions linked to the setback. Whether it's disappointment or anger, these feelings require acknowledgment to move forward. Journaling can be a powerful method for this. Document how you feel and connect it to thoughts about the "Doubter." Recognizing and processing these emotions aids in moving toward acceptance and healing.

3. **Reframe Goals:** Assess whether your goals

align with your current desires and values. Sometimes, setbacks arise from pursuing objectives that no longer resonate with who we are. Take time to redefine what success looks like for you. Create SMART goals—Specific, Measurable, Achievable, Relevant, and Time-bound—that reflect your new insights. This step reinvigorates your direction, motivating you away from the past.

4. **Seek Guidance:** There's wisdom in seeking support during difficult times. Reach out to mentors, friends, or even support groups that can offer insights into overcoming your setback. Whether sharing advice or simply being there to listen, external perspectives can provide a new narrative and inspire actionable solutions.

5. **Create a Plan:** Develop a step-by-step plan for moving forward. Having a clear outline can offer structure, reducing feelings of overwhelm caused by inaction. List actionable steps that align with your reframed goals, and set timelines for completing them. This plan might involve furthering your education, seeking new career opportunities, or even emotional healing practices.

6. **Embrace Resilience:** Resilience is cultivated through practice. Start small and focus on incremental changes that align with your new path. Celebrate each victory along the way, no matter how small. This builds a sense of achievement and reinforces the notion that setbacks can lead to unexpected growth.

Guided Reflection: Evaluating Past CHOICES

To further deepen the understanding of setbacks and how to navigate through them, let's engage in guided reflections. These questions are designed to help you evaluate past CHOICES, drawing lessons rather than focusing on losses.

1. **What was the motivation behind the CHOICE I made?** Reflect on your intentions. Were they driven by external expectations, fear, or genuine aspiration? Gaining insight into your motivations provides clarity about the principles that influence your decision-making.

2. **What consequences did I experience as a result of this CHOICE?** Examine the tangible consequences. What did you lose or gain? Broaden

your perspective to include positive outcomes that may have arisen, even in the face of setbacks.

3.   **What did I learn from this experience?** Shift the focus toward the valuable lessons unearthed from the experience. Consider how it influenced your subsequent decisions.

4.   **How might I make different CHOICES in the future based on this reflection?** Think constructively about how this setback can guide you in making different CHOICES moving forward. What new strategies or mindsets will help avoid similar pitfalls?

5.   **What does success look like to me now?** Create an image of success that resonates with your current self. How has this experience reshaped your vision for the future?

Moving Forward: Embodying Lessons

With profound insights and analyses in hand, it's important to engage in actionable steps that embody the lessons learned from setbacks. The narrative doesn't have to revolve around defeat. Instead, shift the focus toward empowerment through informed CHOICES.

Each setback enhances resilience and reinforces the idea that life is not about avoiding failure but learning to rise after falling. Allow the past to serve as a canvas subject to your unique strokes—each experience is a brushstroke that contributes to a vibrant, multidimensional picture of your life.

As we journey through life's forks in the road, the CHOICES we make—both good and bad—are transformative. Setbacks can lead to groundbreaking insights, urging us to confront our doubts, realign our intentions, and ultimately become better equipped for the myriad CHOICES that lie ahead. By embracing the lessons from setbacks, we paint a future that thrives not on perfection but on continuous growth and self-awareness.

In conclusion, navigating setbacks with courage allows us to face the many forks in the road with renewed confidence and purpose. By harnessing the power of reflection and learning to embrace uncertainty, we are empowered to shape a path that is not merely a response to fear but a proactive engagement with life's abundant opportunities.

The Echo of Past CHOICES

Reflections on CHOICES

In the quiet moments of our lives, when the world falls still and reflective thoughts arise, we find ourselves confronted with the CHOICES that have shaped our narratives. Each decision, whether monumental or seemingly trivial, reverberates through the corridors of time. They are echoes of who we were, who we chose to be, and who we continue to become. As we navigate the complexity of our existence, it becomes essential to pause, to breathe, and to reflect on the

CHOICES of our past that have guided us to this very moment.

CHOICES are not merely opportunities seized or missed; they are, instead, the threads of a tapestry that intertwine our lives with those of others. The cascading impact of our decisions stretches far beyond our immediate context, stitching together connections that span generations. These CHOICES, once made, linger in the atmosphere, reminding us of the inherent power each decision holds. The journeys of our closest friends, our families, and even strangers are altered by the CHOICES we make. Therefore, to reflect meaningfully upon our past is to understand the weight of our decisions.

Take, for instance, the path of a weary traveler. Imagine a young woman named Leah, standing at a crossroads during her college years. She has two options before her: to pursue a lucrative job offer in the city or to follow her passion for humanitarian work overseas. The CHOICE she makes will set in motion a series of events that redefine her life. Leah ultimately chooses to embrace adventure and service, embarking on a journey that changes her perspective on the world. She works with communities in underprivileged areas, fostering relationships and contributing to invaluable projects. However, it is not just Leah who is affected; as she pours her heart into the lives of others, she inadvertently inspires a team of volunteers who join her cause.

Years later, one of those volunteers, Henry, reflects on how Leah's initial CHOICE of service encouraged him to lead a life of giving. Without hesitation, he recalls how her steadfast commitment altered his understanding of purpose. The ripple effect of Leah's decision is writ large in the lives of those she impacted directly, but it continues to unfold in the lives of people like Henry, who carry the torch she ignited through her CHOICE.

Such reflections provoke a contemplative examination: how many CHOICES have we made that have similarly echoed through the lives of others? Each morning, we make a variety of decisions, from what we consume for breakfast to the tone we adopt in our interactions with others. These are the seemingly mundane CHOICES, often overlooked, yet they lie at the foundation of the emotional landscapes we find ourselves in each day.

One might ponder the CHOICE of kindness over indifference. A moment of compassion—speaking a kind word, lending a hand, or offering encouragement—can ignite a transformation in someone who may be quietly battling personal struggles. Consider the story of Raj, who, on a rainy Thursday, decides to forego his usual brisk walk to work and instead stops to share an umbrella with a stranger caught in the downpour. In that brief encounter, he offers not just shelter from the rain but sparks a conversation that renews the stranger's hope in humanity.

The echo of that single CHOICE resonates beyond Raj and the stranger; it influences how the stranger interacts with others later in the day, and they may carry that warmth into their own relationships. A shared umbrella fills a gap in the shared human experience, a reminder that kindness travels through invisible threads connecting us all.

The importance of self-reflection cannot be overstated. It serves as a vessel for deriving meaning from our past. Taking the time to revisit our CHOICES, to acknowledge what has unfolded from those moments, becomes an exercise in understanding ourselves more authentically. In a world bustling with noise and distraction, self-reflection allows us the space to sift through experiences and illuminate the lessons embedded within them.

Let's think about another example—Samantha, a once career-driven executive who dedicated her life to climbing the corporate ladder. Over the years, her CHOICES had led her to power and prestige, yet they came at the cost of her health and relationships. One day, while reflecting on her life during a lonely evening, she realizes that her pursuit of success has led her to isolate herself from loved ones. The CHOICE to chase ambition, although rewarding in status, has echoed a sense of emptiness.

In a moment of profound contemplation, Samantha decides to change course. She begins to prioritize connection over competition, intentionally making CHOICES to restore those relationships. As time unfolds, this decision blossoms into a rich tapestry of love and support, fortifying her spirit in ways material wealth never could. The echoes of her CHOICE breathe life back into her existence, enhancing not only her well-being but also the lives of those around her who benefit from her renewed presence.

This illustrates the dual role our CHOICES play: they can bring us joy and realization, but they may also lead to regret and longing if left unchecked. The weight of our past CHOICES carries the duality of light and shadow. As we shine a light on our past, we resonate with both the good and the bad, which together shape who we are. The wisdom drawn from past experiences can illuminate our path forward, providing insight into how our CHOICES today will echo into the future.

What, then, can be gleaned from the echoes of our decisions? The answer lies within the act of careful introspection. Engage in reflective practices—write in journals, create art, or engage in meaningful conversations with trusted friends. These exercises facilitate understanding, allowing us to analyze past CHOICES, the emotions surrounding them, and the outcomes they elicited. From these reflections, we discover the emotional weight attached to our decisions, illuminating the beauty, pain, triumph, and lessons they encapsulate.

Within the weathered pages of a journal lie our reflections; they frame the landscape of our emotional journeys. A past relationship that sparked love and connection may linger as a sweet memory, while others may echo with the intense pain of heartbreak. Both scenarios provide insight, rich lessons woven through our experiences, guiding us as we face future relationships. By reflecting upon the CHOICES that brought us to both joy and pain, we foster a deeper awareness of our desires, fears, and attributes that enrich our futures.

As we engage with the past and confront our CHOICES

courageously, we allow ourselves to redefine narratives; we can uncover the significance of both the decisions that propelled us forward and those that taught us through adversity. The beauty of CHOICE is not just in the outcomes but in their potential to reveal to us our core values and beliefs.

We often speak of legacy, of the footprints we leave behind; realizing the power of CHOICE among generations approaches the realm of sacred responsibility. The echoes of our CHOICES may resonate not just within us but also through the lives of others in unexpected and profound ways. We are bound together through the moments where our lives intersect, amplifying the significance of intentional decisions.

Picture a grandfather, Joseph, who shared his passion for woodworking with his grandson, Oliver. Joseph chose to spend quality time teaching Oliver how to carve and create beautiful pieces of art from wood. Through these purposeful CHOICES, Joseph imparts valuable skills and life lessons about patience, perseverance, and creativity. Years later, after Joseph's passing, Oliver finds solace in the workshop where they once shared laughter and learning. He carries on his grandfather's legacy, spreading joy by crafting pieces for others while sharing the stories learned from those shared moments.

The resonance of Joseph's CHOICES goes beyond a mere skill transfer; it instills values that underpin Oliver's identity. This kind of legacy, built on intentional CHOICES, flourishes when nurtured with meaningful interactions that lift others up, leading them to emulate those very values in their lives.

In recognizing our CHOICES in this way, we cultivate an understanding that ripples through our existence. It becomes imperative to reflect not just on grand gestures but also on the subtle everyday CHOICES—the seemingly mundane interactions that speak to our character. A whispered apology offered in earnest, an invitation extended, or a listening ear provided during someone's tough moment—these moments may seem small, yet their cumulative effects can lead to transformation.

In the act of reflection, we learn to forgive ourselves for past mistakes, acknowledging that CHOICES made in moments of impulse or fear do not define us. Instead, they contribute to the rich narrative of our lives, one in which we grow and evolve. It is through the act of recognizing our imperfections that we cultivate greater empathy, not only for ourselves but for others, inspiring compassion as we witness their struggles, forged from CHOICES perhaps similar to ours.

Our past, replete with echoes of experiences and CHOICES, undoubtedly shapes our present and future. The exploration of these echoes continues to reveal insights, allowing us to understand our lives more fully. Encourage yourself to linger in those reflections, celebrating the light and navigating the shadows. Each memory, each decision, is a piece of the puzzle that forms your identity, shaping the path before you.

As you stand at the precipice of your memories, consider creating a ritual around self-reflection. Celebrate the stories that have birthed you—each CHOICE an artist's stroke on the canvas of your life. With each act of reflection, may you not only reclaim the beauty embedded within your past but also become a beacon of hope who recognizes that the echoes of your CHOICES can inspire others.

We are invited to share this journey, recognizing that each individual's CHOICES echo through time, creating a collective resounding chord of experiences that unify us. With intention, may we aspire to craft CHOICES that not only define our essence but significantly impact the narrative we share with the world, ensuring that the echoes of our CHOICES resonate in compassionate and empowering ways.

Forging New Paths from the Ruins

In the quiet moments of reflection, when the world seems to fade into the background and only the echoes of our past remain alive, we often confront the heavy weight of our CHOICES. Each decision leaves a mark, etching itself into the fabric of our lives—some as brilliant colors woven into a breathtaking tapestry, while others appear as dark stains or frayed edges, reminders of mistakes we wish we could erase. But what if, instead of viewing our past errors as burdens, we could see them as the very soil from which new growth can emerge? This subchapter invites you to explore the transformative power of self-forgiveness, urging you to rewrite your narrative and forge new paths from the ruins of your past.

Self-forgiveness is not merely a gift we grant ourselves; it is a critical skill that enables us to transcend the echo of our past CHOICES. It allows us to acknowledge our missteps without letting them define who we are. Amid a society that often casts judgment with unwavering resolve, the journey toward self-forgiveness requires courage and vulnerability. It calls us to embrace the lessons hidden within our past, using them as stepping stones toward healing and personal growth.

Embracing this perspective is vital to moving forward, transforming regret into a source of strength and wisdom.

To illustrate the essence of forging new paths, consider the allegory of the phoenix. The mythical bird rises from the ash of its former self, embodying resilience and renewal. This powerful image serves as a reminder that, from the ashes of our past CHOICES, we too can rise anew. Each setback, each moment of failure, carries the potential for rebirth if we allow ourselves to engage deeply with our experiences. This chapter aims to foster that understanding through practical strategies, personal reflections, and transformative exercises designed to cultivate self-forgiveness.

As we embark on this exploration, it is essential to acknowledge that the journey toward self-forgiveness is deeply personal. It varies from one individual to another, shaped by unique experiences, emotions, and perceptions. Thus, the first step is to create a safe space for yourself—a sacred space where you can reflect openly and honestly about your past CHOICES without fear of judgment or criticism.

Creating Your Sacred Space

Find a quiet place, free from distractions, where you feel comfortable and safe. This might be a cozy corner of your home, a seat on a park bench overlooking a tranquil lake, or even a favorite spot in nature. Bring along a journal or a sheet of paper and your preferred writing tool. Take a few deep breaths to center yourself, allowing any tension to melt away. As you settle into your sacred space, invite clarity and openness into your thoughts. What past CHOICES come to mind? What emotions arise as you reflect on them?

Once you've created this environment, it's time to give voice to those echoes. Write down the CHOICES you regret or the actions that left you feeling less than proud. Allow the words to flow freely, without self-editing. Let your heart guide your pen.

Next, identify the lesson hidden within each experience. What did you learn about yourself? Were there patterns that you can now recognize? Perhaps you see that in a relationship, you failed to set boundaries, or you ventured into a career that didn't align with your values. Document these insights alongside your reflections. Recognizing the lessons learned is crucial, as they become the foundation upon which you build new narratives.

Once you've mapped your regrets and their associated lessons, let's delve into the core philosophy of redemption and self-forgiveness. These concepts intertwine beautifully, revealing a path toward personal growth. Redemption does not mean erasing the past; instead, it signifies acknowledging the full spectrum of experiences—both light and dark—and choosing to learn and grow from them.

Understanding the Concept of Redemption

Redemption invites us to transform pain into purpose, guiding our actions toward a deeper understanding of ourselves and our impact on the world. It encourages us to recognize that our failures do not diminish our worth but rather enhance our humanity. Every individual has made CHOICES that they wish they could undo, and yet it is through these experiences that we cultivate empathy, resilience, and strength.

To solidify this understanding, reflect on a pivotal moment in your life where you felt the weight of your CHOICE pressing down on you. Perhaps it was a harsh word spoken in anger, a decision that led to a relationship's end, or a career change that didn't quite work out. Now consider how that moment, albeit painful, shaped your path. What values do you hold dear now as a result? How have your perspectives shifted?

After contemplating these questions, write a short letter to your past self. Address the version of you that made that CHOICE, pouring out your thoughts and feelings with compassion. Let them know that while the decision may have seemed monumental at the time, the journey you've walked since has contributed to who you are today—a wiser, more resilient individual. Offer yourself forgiveness. This exercise can be a transformative gesture, helping you embody the self-compassion necessary for healing.

Practical Exercises for Self-Forgiveness

1.   **Journaling Reflection:** Dedicate consistent time for this practice. Each week, select one regret and explore it through writing. Begin with a description of the CHOICE, then transition into understanding its impact. Follow with a section devoted to the lessons learned and the steps you can take moving forward.

2.   **Affirmations of Forgiveness:** Craft affirmations that resonate with your healing journey. For example, "I forgive myself for my past mistakes; they have taught me valuable lessons." Repeat these affirmations daily, allowing their power to sink deep into your convictions.

3.   **Creating a Forgiveness Ritual:** Design a personal ritual that embodies your commitment to self-forgiveness.

This could involve lighting a candle, engaging in meditation, or performing a symbolic act of release—such as writing your regrets on paper and safely burning them, watching as they turn to ash, and with it, your connection to that pain.

4.   **Cultivating Gratitude:** Recognize the beauty within your journey by engaging in a gratitude practice. At the end of each day, note three things that you appreciate about yourself or your experiences, including those that seemed negative at the time. This will shift your focus from regret to appreciation, fostering self-love.

5.   **Engaging in Healing Conversations:** Seek out a trusted friend, mentor, or therapist, and share the burdens of your past CHOICES. Engage in a dialogue that honors vulnerability, allowing that person to reflect back to you the strength they see that may have been obscured by your self-doubt. Sharing our stories can be profoundly liberating; it reframes our experiences in a supportive light.

Shaping Powerful Narratives Moving Forward

Now that we have established the foundations of self-forgiveness and explored actionable exercises, let's discuss the crucial aspect of shaping powerful new narratives. Every moment provides us with the chance to redefine our future.

Our past does not dictate us; rather, it enriches the complex story we write each day.

Consider crafting a new narrative around a particular regret. Imagine taking the lessons learned and incorporating them as guiding stars on your journey moving ahead. What can you envision for yourself as you step into this new chapter? Write this future narrative in detail:

- What are your intentions?

- What actions will you take to align with your values?

- How will you react differently when faced with similar CHOICES?

This narrative should be vibrant and aspirational, embodying the direction you wish your life to take. Post it somewhere visible—a mirror, a journal, or even as a screensaver on your devices. Allow it to serve as a constant reminder of the path you are forging, one where the ruins of the past serve merely as a foundation for a brighter future.

Embracing the Ongoing Journey of Forgiveness

Remember that self-forgiveness is not a one-time event; it is an ongoing journey. You may find yourself revisiting past

CHOICES periodically, grappling with feelings of guilt or shame anew. During these moments, returning to the practices and exercises we've explored in this subchapter will anchor you in your commitment to personal growth.

As you navigate this complex terrain, remind yourself that every individual is a work in progress. Resilience lies not in perfection but in authentic expression and growth amidst our imperfections. When we allow ourselves the grace to learn from our errors, we open the door to a richer, deeper connection—not only with ourselves but with others as well.

Finally, it is worthwhile to remember that the journey of self-forgiveness, like any other profound endeavor, is enriched when shared. Encourage others in your life to embark on this journey alongside you or share the principles of forgiveness you have come to embrace. In doing so, you create a supportive community that recognizes the beauty of transformation.

The Community of Forgiveness

There is strength in numbers, and healing is often amplified within a community environment. Consider gathering friends or family to engage in collective discussions about CHOICES, mistakes, and paths toward self-forgiveness. Shared stories may unlock insights, compassion, and understanding, allowing participants to witness both the struggle and the beauty of others' journeys.

Encourage group activities, such as art projects where participants express their feelings about past CHOICES, fostering a collective atmosphere of understanding and acceptance. Collaborative dynamics can be an incubator for growth, empowering everyone to rise from the ashes together.

Emerging from the ruins of our past not only revitalizes our own narratives but also strengthens the foundations we lay for future generations. As you embrace the tenets of self-forgiveness, remember that your journey is a testament to resilience—the flames of your past may have burned, but from those ashes, a strength has been reborn.

In conclusion, embrace this journey wholeheartedly. Take action, and allow the lessons from your CHOICES to guide you. Root yourself in the fertile soil of forgiveness, drawing strength from it to forge new paths that celebrate life's intricate beauty.

As you step confidently onto the road ahead, remember that you are creating a narrative of courage, resilience, and unconditional love—a tale to be cherished, shared, and celebrated as part of the rich tapestry of humanity.

Legacy of CHOICES Made

In this intricate dance of life, CHOICES made serve as ripples in an ever-expanding pond, altering not just our own paths but also the landscapes of those who follow us. The weight of individual decisions often feels solitary; the moments of CHOICE might be fleeting, decisions wrapped up in the humdrum of life. Yet, through the lens of time, what emerges is a tapestry of interconnected legacies, enduring narratives shaped by countless CHOICES. This exploration invites us to recognize not only the CHOICES we have made but also the profound impact they can yield across generations.

From the moment we take our first breath, our lives are defined by moments of CHOICE. Each decision lays down a thread in the expansive fabric of our existence. These threads form a story, a narrative that extends beyond the self, influencing the lives of those we love and care for. The echo of our CHOICES reverberates through time, carried by familial ties, friendships, and even the communities we inhabit. As we navigate through life, the stories we create and the legacies we forge become a means of connection—not just to our pasts, but to our futures.

The concept of a legacy is often viewed through a lens of monumental achievements: landmarks, charitable foundations, literary masterpieces. While these can be compelling, they overlook the quieter, yet no less powerful, legacies shaped by daily decisions and interpersonal connections. The whispers of love, the quiet acts of kindness, and the lessons learned through hardship contribute significantly to the rich tapestry of what we leave behind. These minutiae craft the essence of who we are and shape what we pass on to those coming after us.

Consider the simple yet profound CHOICES our parents made long before we arrived in the world. For example, a mother's decision to instill values of compassion in her children can reverberate through generations, encouraging future grandchildren to extend kindness wherever they go. Small decisions on how one reacts in times of adversity— whether to harbor resentment or choose forgiveness—impact not only one's personal narrative but also cascade through the lives of those within their influence.

Vignettes of familial experiences further illuminate this theme, offering us snapshots of how CHOICE shapes legacy. Picture a grandmother who, during the Great Depression, chooses to share her meager resources with neighbors rather than hoard them. This act of generosity, though small in the grand narrative of history, creates a legacy of compassion that defines her family for generations. Her children learn to prioritize community and care over accumulation, passing this wisdom to their descendants, who continue to extend their hands to help others. The CHOICES made in moments of economic crisis become the bedrock of familial values, shaping identities and relationships.

We can look to countless stories across families and cultures, where every CHOICE made—whether small or grand—stitches into the collective fabric of identity. There are fathers who choose to spend evenings reading to their children rather than watching television, imparting knowledge and nurturing imagination. Mothers who choose to forgive betrayals teach their children the strength that comes from compassion over vengeance. Each of these decisions, though ordinary on its own, becomes integral to a legacy steeped in wisdom, empathy, and understanding.

The contrast in CHOICES made also reveals profound lessons in legacy. In families where generations have chosen distrust and resentment, there often lies a tangled history of disconnection, pain, and misunderstanding. The lessons learned from these familial narratives can be stark. Children exposed to these legacies of division may grow up carrying the weight of unresolved frustrations, shaping their decisions in ways that perpetuate the cycle of strife. However, recognizing this cycle grants the possibility of transformation. When an individual in such a lineage chooses to buck the trend, to forge a new narrative of healing and communication, an entirely different legacy is initiated.

As we reflect on our personal CHOICES, it becomes necessary to project how those CHOICES connect to the broader historical narrative. What do we want our stories to contribute to the tapestry of humanity? We exist within a continuum; our actions today set the wheels in motion for narratives not yet written. For instance, if a parent chooses to prioritize education and instill a love of learning in their children, the ripples can touch an entire generation of scholars, thinkers, and visionaries. A simple, yet crucial, CHOICE to value knowledge over ignorance can literally shape a community's future.

Moreover, it isn't merely about the CHOICES we actively make; sometimes, the legacy of unmade CHOICES also beckons our reflection. When we choose inaction—silencing our convictions or allowing doubts to curtail our dreams—the echoes can be just as resonant. They may create lives marked by missed opportunities. Reflecting on these can be painful, but it also offers incredible insight into the nature of our legacies, grounding us in the understanding that while we cannot change the past, we can illuminate the paths forward with consciousness and intention.

Creating a meaningful legacy requires conscious effort, a deliberate CHOICE to strive for a connection that spans beyond our immediate desires. It involves engaging with our ancestry and recognizing the threads that connect us to those who came before. This engagement fosters integrity and belonging, allowing us to stand upon the foundation built by the CHOICES of our forebears even as we extend the narrative with our unique struggles and triumphs.

As you contemplate your own legacy, think of the CHOICES you plan to make moving forward. When a commitment is made to live intentionally, the narrative shifts. Embrace the vibrancy of CHOICE as a tool for creation rather than an obstacle to be feared. The consequences of our CHOICES will define not just our lives but also the hearts and minds of those who come after us. Thus, we are called to foster conversations about legacy, not only to inquire about our points of impact but also to invite others into that space of reflection.

As you gather around the table with family, foster dialogues about your shared histories. Ask, "What CHOICES shaped our family? What dreams remain unfulfilled? How can we alter the conversation of legacy moving forward?" These discussions open up pathways to healing, shared understanding, and ultimately the legacy of stronger connections among family members.

And when it comes time to impart wisdom to the younger generations, entrust them with the weight of their CHOICES. Encourage them to honor the legacy of love, resilience, and generosity of spirit. It is vital to frame the discussions around CHOICE as a sacred gift—an opportunity to shape not only personal narratives but societal narratives as well.

In order to visualize the legacy we wish to leave behind, imagine standing at the shore of a lake, the still waters reflecting all that has been and all that could be. Each ripple that spreads affects the shoreline, drawing together grains of sand and pebbles that rid themselves of isolation. Legacy emerges much in the same way. Every moment of CHOICE, every act of kindness or indifference, adds to the rich depth of the waters that define our existence, touching upon the edges of others' lives, resonating with familiarity and warmth.

All this comes together in the recognition that our CHOICES do carry weight; they can shape entire histories and futures. What remains is the understanding that legacy is not just what one leaves behind but the impact they create in motion. Therefore, as you reflect on your past CHOICES, consider how they illuminate the path ahead. The legacy you build is always growing, always taking shape as you carve your path into existence.

Finally, consider your own legacy as a continuously evolving narrative, a story that interweaves your dreams, struggles, and triumphs with the dreams, struggles, and triumphs of those who came before and those who will come after. Reflect on how the CHOICES you make today can serve as a benediction for future generations. Hold close the understanding that the legacy of CHOICES made is not a burden, but a profound gift—a thread that binds you, your family, and future generations together in an extravagant tapestry of life.

The Weight of Regret

Understanding Regret

Regret, a profoundly human emotion, often arrives quietly, almost uninvited, only to settle heavily around our shoulders like a thick, unbearable cloak. It carries with it a weight that can both shield and suffocate, offering warmth in its familiarity yet stifling in its persistence. Regret is not merely a reflection of past decisions; it is a visceral reminder of the CHOICES we have made—and perhaps those we didn't make—and the consequences that inevitably followed. As we navigate the complex terrain of life, recognizing and understanding regret can enable us to transform those burdens into stepping stones on our journey toward growth and authenticity.

Many of us find ourselves standing at the crossroads of CHOICES, contemplating which path to pursue. Whether it is a decision about a career, a relationship, or even a fleeting moment that seemed inconsequential at the time, the CHOICES we make leave lasting imprints on our lives. Once made, those CHOICES can linger in our minds, replaying in an endless loop, providing fertile ground for self-reflection—yet also for self-recrimination. This intricate interplay of CHOICE and regret demands our attention.

Consider the experience of a young woman named Anna. At twenty-four, she was graduating from college, filled with dreams and aspirations. Anna had a CHOICE to make: accept a job offer with a well-known company in her field or embark on a once-in-a-lifetime backpacking trip across Europe with her friends. After much deliberation, she chose the job, believing it was the "responsible" decision. Months later, as she sat in an unfulfilling meeting, the weight of her regret became palpable. Every time a friend posted pictures of their adventures abroad, she felt the cloak of regret tighten around her shoulders, reminding her of the freedom she had let slip through her fingers.

Anna's story resonates with many; it is a prime example of how regret can manifest in the everyday CHOICES that seem monumental at the time. The burden of regret often feels heavy, full of questions that echo in the mind: What if I had chosen differently? What would my life look like now? These questions remain persistent, ensnaring us in a cycle of what-ifs and should-haves, reminding us of the roads not taken. As we delve deeper into the nature of regret, it becomes apparent that it is more than just an emotional response; it is a signal that serves a purpose.

Regret teaches us about our values and desires. It exposes the discrepancies between who we are and who we wish to become. In Anna's case, her CHOICE reflected a commitment to societal expectations rather than her own long-held desires for adventure and exploration. Each time regret clothed her in discontent, it nudged her toward reevaluation—setting the stage for personal growth.

Regret also has a peculiar way of intertwining with our identities. We might find ourselves saying things like, "I regret that I never took the opportunity to travel, and now I am the type of person who stays in one place." This self-labeling can create a prison of our own making, confining us to an identity shaped solely by past decisions rather than our potential for future change. Each regret can cast shadows over our self-image and influence how we perceive ourselves in various contexts, molding our narratives in unintentional ways.

Within the tapestry of our lives, the threads of regret create unique patterns. Some individuals experience healthy regret, which leads to introspection and growth. They learn from past decisions and make different CHOICES in the future. Others carry regret as a heavy burden, allowing it to define them instead of using it as a means to educate themselves. In understanding the nature of regret, we are given the option to choose how to interact with our own feelings of disappointment.

Consider the perspective of Michael, a once-aspiring musician who had always dreamed of sharing his music with the world. He reached a pivotal moment when he had the opportunity to perform at a local venue that could catapult his career. Instead of taking the stage, fear held him back, and he declined. Years passed, and as he watched others, including friends, achieve success, he often felt crushed under the weight of unmet aspirations. Regret lived in the tiny moments—the missed opportunities transformed into mental labels: "a coward," "an underachiever," "someone who never took a risk."

Michael's experience illustrates how regret can be a double-edged sword. It can be paralyzing, but it can also serve as a catalyst for change. The key lies in our response. If we allow regret to consume us, defining who we are based on our past CHOICES, we create a chasm that separates us from the identities we aspire to embody. This internal struggle prompts us to ask critical questions about the narrative we create for ourselves.

Through the lens of those who have encountered regret, we see a mosaic of emotions—sadness, frustration, anger, and sometimes, unexpectedly, gratitude. For many, the essential lessons learned from regrettable decisions illuminate paths that have ultimately led to personal evolution. As we delve deeper, it becomes evident that while the weight of regret can feel burdensome, there is potential for enlightenment within that heaviness.

Rachel, another individual who has danced with regret, found herself at an intersection of relationships. In her early thirties, she chose a stable partnership instead of pursuing her passion for art. Over the years, as the walls of her life grew confining, she felt increasingly stifled without the creative outlet that once brought her happiness. Upon reflecting on her CHOICES, Rachel recognized that the decision to prioritize stability over passion had cost her much more than a fleeting moment of security. In hindsight, this CHOICE cultivated a deeper understanding of her own desires. While regret hung around her like a cloud, it soon cleared, unveiling the creativity she longed to express.

The journey through regret can indeed be transformational. It is not merely about self-blame but about uncovering insights. Each experience presents an opportunity to learn and grow, allowing us to repurpose regret into wisdom that can drive future CHOICES. What stands out in Rachel's story is her realization of the importance of staying connected with her inner self; it is this connection that ultimately allows her to emerge from her regrets renewed and inspired.

In examining the emotional toll of regret, we should also consider the impact it has on our relationships with others. Regret can be a solitary experience, yet it also intertwines with the lives of those we love. When we harbor regret, it can lead to distance and disconnection. It becomes a clog in the stream of relationship dynamics, often making us feel like we are living in a shadowy existence rather than fully engaging in life with joy and authenticity. For instance, Anna's regret over her career CHOICE led to feelings of jealousy toward her friends who traveled, causing her to withdraw and retreat into herself. The emotional burden created a distance that impacted her relationships, leading her to feel more isolated—a cycle that likely compounds the regret itself.

Navigating through the terrain of regret beckons us toward empathy, both for ourselves and for those around us. Each individual carries their own regrets, often hidden behind smiles or subdued laughter. Working collectively toward a broader understanding of regret can create a nurturing environment where vulnerability is embraced. When we engage in heartfelt conversations about regret, we embark on a journey that leads to authenticity, allowing us to uncloak the heaviness that encircles us.

Delving into regret compels us to wrestle with emotions that may be uncomfortable. It is often easy to dismiss regret as a sign of weakness or failure; however, it embodies our humanity. By acknowledging regret, we embrace the intricacies of our CHOICES, the breath of possibility that still exists beyond the weight we carry. As we undertake this introspective journey, it becomes clear that regret is not the end of our narrative but rather a significant thread in our existence—a guide that helps illuminate our path as we continue to forge ahead.

The understanding of regret must extend beyond the personal realm into the shared experiences of our communities. In a world where CHOICES constantly ripple through the lives of others, our regrets can influence the collective as much as they affect the individual. This awareness invites us to accept the moral responsibility that accompanies our CHOICES. It beckons us to consider how our decisions, and the regrets that might stem from them, create echoes that can affect those around us—whether positively or negatively.

Through the lens of regret, we can cultivate empathy that transcends mere understanding. We transition from a mindset of judgment to one of compassion. This is particularly profound when we consider the broader narratives surrounding regret, such as the CHOICES that lead to systemic injustices, detrimental patterns within family structures, or individual decisions that ripple through generations. Harnessing an empathetic approach, we can foster healing conversations and supportive actions that nurture growth and understanding.

As we conclude our exploration of regret, it is essential to remember that regret can be our greatest teacher. Just as Anna, Michael, and Rachel learned to interrogate the narratives their regrets anchored them to, so can we. The heavy cloak of regret may weigh us down, but instead of allowing it to immobilize us, we have the power to transform that weight into wings of wisdom. What remains is an ongoing process of engagement with the CHOICES we make—both past and future—inviting us to craft narratives that reflect our evolving selves, free from the suffocating shadows of regret.

The burden of unfulfilled CHOICES can act as both an anchor and a compass, guiding us toward authenticity. In embracing the lessons regret offers, we are empowered to choose differently in our journeys ahead. Rather than allowing regret to define us, let it ignite passion and resilience within, propelling us toward the potential awaiting on the horizon of our tomorrows.

In our quest to understand regret, we recognize it for what it is—a profound expression of our humanity, a testament to our complexity, and a doorway to the transformational power of CHOICE. With each step we take, as we choose to confront our regrets, we embark on a journey of reflection, growth, and a deeper understanding of what it means to navigate the intricate tapestry of our lives.

Transforming Regret into Fuel

Regret is a complex emotion, often intertwined with feelings of sadness, disappointment, and sometimes even shame. It hovers like a shadow in our minds, tugging at us when we least expect it. We find ourselves replaying certain moments, stuck in the grip of what could have been. Yet, as daunting as it may seem, regret can also be the catalyst for profound transformation. In this subchapter, we delve into the art of converting regret into fuel for motivation and change, illuminating a path toward redemption.

Shifting Perspectives on Regret

To effectively transform regret into fuel, we must first shift our perspective. Rather than viewing regret solely as a burden, we can begin to see it as an opportunity for learning and growth. Regret signifies that we have aspirations, dreams, and standards for ourselves. It serves as a reminder of our values and desires, urging us to realign with the path we wish to take.

Consider the moments in your life that you deeply regret. What do these events reveal about your values? Perhaps you regret not pursuing a particular career. This sentiment might illuminate your passion for creativity or your desire for

121

meaningful work. By unpacking the emotion tied to regret, you can uncover the motivations that can propel you forward.

When we change our mindset from dwelling on regret to exploring its meanings, we start to gather the lessons it imparts. This reframing is a crucial first step in transforming regret into something constructive. Instead of allowing regret to paralyze us, we must embrace it, acknowledge its presence, and then reclaim its power to ignite change.

The Power of Reflection: Journaling Exercises

One of the most effective tools we can use in this journey of transformation is reflection through writing. Journaling helps us process our emotions, clearing mental clutter and allowing the lessons of regret to rise to the surface. Below are several journaling prompts designed to facilitate this exploration:

1. **Identify Your Regrets**: Write about the specific incidents or decisions that you regret. Which CHOICES weigh heavily on your heart? Be as descriptive and honest as possible.

2. **Explore the Why**: For each regret, explore why it bothers you. What did you hope to achieve? What values were violated? Understanding the roots of these regrets can illuminate areas of your life that need addressing.

3.   **Lessons Learned**: Reflect on what each regret has taught you. Even if the lesson is painful, find a way to articulate its significance. How has this regret shaped your beliefs or intentions?

4.   **Reframe the Narrative**: Rewrite the story associated with your regret. Instead of viewing it as a failure, present it as a learning experience. How might this regret serve as a guiding pillar in your future decisions?

5.   **Actionable Steps**: Identify three actionable steps you can take to transform each regret into something positive. These steps could include reaching out to someone you've wronged, pursuing a dream you set aside, or making a commitment to live by your values.

Harnessing Emotional Energy

Regret carries a unique emotional weight that can, if channeled correctly, be transformed into a powerful driving force for change. Recognize that the energy behind regret, when embraced, can motivate you to set new goals and pursue fresh paths. Consider this:

- **Sparking Change**: Allow the discomfort associated with regret to spark a sense of urgency within you. Use this emotional energy to propel yourself into action, treating it as a signpost for necessary changes in your life.

- **Creating Momentum**: Small actions taken as a result of embracing regret can create momentum. Each step forward reinforces your ability to transform negativity into productivity.

- **Acknowledge the Journey**: Remember that this is not about erasing regret but about honoring the journey it has taken you on. Celebrate the small wins and hold space for your emotions.

Transformational Stories

To illustrate the potential for transformation, let's explore a few stories of individuals who have successfully harnessed their regrets to fuel positive change:

Story 1: Lisa's Second Chance

Lisa found herself in a successful career, yet she couldn't shake the feeling of regret for not pursuing her passion for painting. The years passed, and her brushes gathered dust while her dreams felt dormant. One day, she sat with her journal and confronted her regret. Acknowledging her suppressed passion led her to enroll in a local art class, where she discovered the joy of creation once more. Lisa's journey transformed her life; not only did she regain her artistic happiness, but she also started a small business selling her artwork, allowing her to connect with others through her passion.

Story 2: Mark's Reconciliation

Mark faced deep regret over a severed relationship with his father, stemming from an argument that led to years of silence. After years of carrying this regret, Mark decided to confront it through journaling. He wrote letters he never sent and finally found the courage to reach out. Through a heartfelt conversation, he and his father were able to heal and reconnect. This act of courage shifted Mark's entire outlook on relationships, inspiring him to foster more open communication with those he loved. Regret transformed into resolution, and their bond grew stronger than ever.

Building a New Identity

As we harness regret into fuel, we also lay the groundwork for constructing a new identity—one rooted in resilience and the courage to face our emotional landscapes. Here are some strategies to aid in this rebuilding:

1. **Embrace Vulnerability**: Accept that it is okay to feel

regret and that confronting these feelings is essential for growth. Vulnerability allows you to connect more deeply with yourself and others, fostering a sense of belonging.

2. **Establish New Goals**: Allow your reflections to guide you in forming new intentions and goals. Whether these are related to personal growth, career paths, or relationships, establishing concrete steps can provide clarity and motivation.

3. **Seek Support**: Surround yourself with supportive individuals who encourage your journey toward transformation. Sometimes sharing your regrets with those you trust can lighten the load and open the door for collaborative healing.

4. **Practice Self-Compassion**: Remind yourself that everyone has regrets; it is part of being human. Cultivating self-compassion will allow you to forgive yourself more readily and move forward with clarity and purpose.

5. **Visualize the Future**: Take time to visualize what your life can look like beyond your regrets. Picture yourself having transformed pain into purpose; what does that future hold? Create a vision board or mind map that embodies your aspirations.

Actioning Insights

Ultimately, the goal is action. After reflecting and journaling, the next phase is putting insights into practice. Here are a few actionable steps to kickstart this transformation:

•   **Set Mini Goals**: Break down broader goals into smaller, manageable actions. This approach prevents overwhelm and offers a clear path toward change.

•   **Accountability Partners**: Share your action plan with a trusted friend or mentor who can hold you accountable. Regular check-ins can help you maintain your momentum and celebrate your progress.

•   **Reflect Regularly**: Make it a habit to revisit your regrets and the steps you are taking to transform them. This might include monthly check-ins to track your emotional growth and goal completion.

Conclusion: The Transformation Process

Regret, while painful, need not be a permanent fixture in our lives. By shifting our perspective, harnessing the emotional energy tied to regret, and taking actionable steps toward change, we can transform what once pulled us down into a powerful engine for personal growth.

In this journey, acknowledge that healing may not be linear; it's filled with ebbs and flows, moments of doubt, and bursts of clarity. As you navigate this path, remember that you are not alone—many have walked this road before you, and they too have come to understand the profound potential that lies within embracing their regrets.

As you step into the future, you hold the capacity to take charge of your story. Use regret as a driving force that propels you toward realization and fulfillment, continually moving you toward the life you've envisioned—a life rich with intention, purpose, and transformative growth.

The Burden of Unmade CHOICES

The tangible weight of unmade CHOICES can be more burdensome than the aftermath of decisions made in haste. Each CHOICE we face is a crossroad, a moment that could potentially pivot the course of our lives. Yet, there exists a subtle shadow cast by the decisions we never enacted—the paths we never traversed, the voices we never listened to, the dreams we never chased. Burdened by the echoes of these unmade CHOICES, it's essential to turn our gaze inward and contemplate the fears that paralyze our decision-making process.

In our society, there's an almost romanticized notion of regret tied to the concept of living boldly. But when we truly examine the essence of regret, we uncover a much deeper conflict between desire and fear. It's not merely the fear of failure, but a more complex web interwoven with insecurities, societal expectations, and the silent murmurs of self-doubt. Each of these threads can shackle our ambition, leading to friction and resistance when faced with the crossroads of potential.

Reflect for a moment on a time in your life when you stood at an important junction. There you were, acknowledging two diverging paths. One beckoned with familiarity and safety, while the other shimmered with the promise of unknown adventure but was obscured by formidable fears. More often than not, it was the fear that led you to retreat into the comfort of inaction. The potential for unfulfilled dreams hangs heavily upon our hearts in such moments.

Many of us can vividly remember periods in our lives when we hesitated to speak up, to express our true feelings, or to pursue that nagging aspiration that whispered frequently in the stillness. Was there a job you dreamed of applying for but sensed an obstacle in your way? Did you see an opportunity to deepen a relationship but let it slip through your fingers?

Perhaps it was a desire to travel solo, but fear held you back from stepping into foreign lands alone. These instances carry an emotional weight that stays with us and strains our consciousness, a weight no different from that of regret.

Fear, in its myriad forms—fear of judgment, fear of the unknown, fear of abandoning comfort—works insidiously, creeping in like a fog that blurs our vision and grips our heart. It tells us to play small, to adhere to the ordinary, and that stepping out of our comfort zone could lead to disaster. Nevertheless, every day we let fear dictate our CHOICES is another day we relinquish the power to shape our own destinies.

To understand the burden of unmade CHOICES, we must first acknowledge fear's role in paralyzing our potential. What drives us to abandon dreams, to not even try? More profoundly, what narratives do we hold within us that reinforce these fears?

Engage in a moment of introspection. Close your eyes and visualize an unmade CHOICE, one that lingers in the recesses of your memory. Allow the emotions associated with that CHOICE to surface: was it regret, sadness, frustration, or a twinge of nostalgia? As you breathe deeply, consider this question: What fears were at play during that moment of inaction?

Having identified these fears, brave the next step of examining their nature. Let's take stock of the fears that often paralyze many as they stand at the gates of change. Public perception plays a pivotal role in many individuals' decisions. The desire to fit in and be accepted can be a deafening voice that drowns out the quieter calls of our ambitions. Reflect on moments when you chose not to pursue an interest—perhaps an art class, a new skill, or even expressing your opinion— because you worried about how you would be perceived. These fears manifest deeply in our psyche, slowing us down and urging caution, but in doing so, they churn up feelings of frustration and, ultimately, regret.

Next, there is the fear of failure. Failing, in many cultures, evokes a strong sense of shame. We are conditioned to seek success, to propagate the narrative of victory. This stems from a societal framework that often fawns over winners while sidelining those who dare to take risks and fail. The anticipated sting of disappointment can feel unbearable, leading us to opt out of opportunities altogether. What might you have gained had you embraced those risks despite the fear? Were there friendships, learning experiences, or rewards that you missed due to those fears?

It's also important to recognize the fear of the unknown. This fear lingers at the edges of our potential. Stepping outside the known path, the one that is familiar and comfortable, can bring about a sense of instability. The unknown—filled with both excitement and anxiety—can invoke a deep-seated aversion. It creates a barrier that claims many dreams before they ever take flight. Have there been dream destinations on your list that you never visited because of this fear? Have relationships been neglected because pursuing them felt too daunting? Recognizing these fears forces a confrontation with the uncomfortable realities we tend to shield ourselves from.

The next step in this journey of understanding the burden of unmade CHOICES is to bring awareness to what kinds of actions can help move beyond these paralyzing fears. There is a distinct power in acknowledging our fears. It is in recognition that we begin to gain traction toward confronting them. One approach to dismantling the paralyzing influence of fear is to cultivate a mindset rooted in potential growth and possibility. This can be achieved through intentional exercises aimed at clarifying your personal wants and dreams.

Begin by creating space for yourself to write. Grab a journal and carve out a few quiet moments in your day when you can engage in reflection. Ask yourself: What dreams have been tucked away in the back of your mind? What would your life look like if you dared to entertain the idea of pursuing these desires? Write down your aspirations, no matter how far-fetched or unattainable they may seem.

Once listed, take a few moments to rate these aspirations according to feasibility and importance to you. Which dreams excite you the most? Which ones evoke a feeling of longing? Not all unmade CHOICES will hold the same significance in your journey, and that's perfectly all right. Choose to focus primarily on the aspirations that resonate deeply with your core values.

Next, consider the fears that may stand in the way of realizing these dreams. For each aspiration listed, express the feelings of fear that emerge. Identify the specific thoughts that your fears convey. Are they messages of inadequacy? Are they exaggerations of potential obstacles? Write them down and then take a moment of gratitude for their presence; they are merely messengers, not the authority of your outcome.

From here, disarm these fears by reframing your internal narrative. Replace limiting beliefs with affirming ones. For instance, instead of saying, "I could never do that," replace it with, "If I take one small step toward it, I could learn and grow." Shifting perspective allows us to weaken the grip that fear holds over our lives.

Next, consider taking actionable mini-steps toward your aspirations. Often, the vision of a grand dream can be intimidating, but breaking it down into manageable chunks paves the way toward progress. Take a single step that aligns with your desire—perhaps a phone call to an old friend, signing up for that course, or simply taking a moment to show kindness to yourself in your journey.

Remember, the process of living authentically involves experimentation. Each step taken can lead to uncharted territory ripe with new experiences, reinforced connections, and growth. Embrace the uncertainty because it is within those moments that the real journey of discovery begins.

As you engage in this process of discovery, remain mindful of one crucial insight: unmade CHOICES do not have to define your path forward. Yes, the ghosts of missed opportunities can cast a heavy aura, but they can also serve as informative beacons guiding your next steps. Reflect upon what those unmade CHOICES have taught you—the attributes they highlight about your character and your values.

Holding space for self-forgiveness becomes paramount, as well. It is easy to chastise ourselves for decisions we didn't pursue, but something remarkable can emerge when we shift toward understanding. Understand that those CHOICES were made in alignment with where you were at that time in life; your development continues to flourish now, too. The burden of unmade CHOICES can be seen as a weight we carry, but as we learn to navigate our fears and strengths, we can transform that weight into a source of wisdom, illuminating the path forward.

Finally, as you traverse this reflective journey, consider initiating conversations with trusted friends or family members about their own unmade CHOICES. Sharing stories fosters connections and reminds us that we are not alone in our struggles. Everyone carries the weight of CHOICES not made, and gathering insight and support can illuminate the path to understanding.

In conclusion, the burden of unmade CHOICES can often feel insurmountable, echoing disappointments that might hinder our perception of our potential. However, by recognizing the fears that inhibit us and reframing our experiences, we can cultivate a mindset centered on possibility and intention. Acknowledge that every CHOICE made and every unmade CHOICE contributes to the tapestry of our lives. With each thread woven, we have the power to trust our journey, embrace new opportunities, and transform the burden of inaction into a celebration of growth, connection, and authenticity.

A Dance with Fear

Fear as a Companion

In the vast landscape of our emotional experiences, fear stands out as a companion that often shadows our CHOICES. It is not merely an obstacle; it is a persistent presence, whispering doubts and concerns into our minds as we navigate through the complex maze of life's decisions. To understand fear fully in this context is to acknowledge it—not as a foe to be vanquished but as an inherent part of the human experience, one we can eventually learn to dance with rather

137

than flee from.

Consider the moment before a significant CHOICE arises—the hushed uncertainty that blankets the air, a kind of stillness that precedes the storm of potential consequences. In these moments, fear often personifies itself as an alter ego; it wears many masks and speaks in various tones. Sometimes, it gently nudges at our conscience, reminding us of the risks we take. Other times, it roars, filling our hearts with dread. Think for a moment: how many times have you stood at the crossroads of decision-making, feeling your pulse quicken, sweat gathering on your palms, as fear gripped you tightly?

Fear's presence is universal, crossing all boundaries of culture, age, and background. It arises in myriad forms—fear of failure, fear of judgment, fear of the unknown—but regardless of its manifestation, it remains an inevitable companion on our journey. The essence of fear is not to paralyze us; instead, it can be viewed as an instinctive response, alerting us to potential danger and prompting us to evaluate our CHOICES critically. Daniel, a recent college graduate, found himself grappling with this very conundrum as he faced the prospect of entering the workforce.

As he prepared for job interviews, feelings of inadequacy

crept into his mind. Would companies value what he had to offer? Would he be able to keep pace in an environment that rewarded experience over potential? With every passing day, fear morphed into a shadowy figure, looming over Daniel and whispering discouragement. He felt frozen, staring at the computer screen filled with job listings, unable to push forward.

But when he quieted the noise of fear, he realized it offered him an invaluable lesson: this whisper of doubt directed him to prepare more thoroughly. Instead of succumbing to paralysis, he began to research companies, tailor his résumé to emphasize his strengths, and practice interview questions with friends. Fear, while uncomfortable, took on a new shape; it became a catalyst for growth and an impetus to action rather than a barrier to it.

Awareness of fear can illuminate what truly matters, guiding us to tap into our core motivations and desires. As we encounter fear with more familiarity, we glean insights about ourselves that deepen our understanding of our ambitions and aspirations.

Fear can be a teacher, revealing our values and priorities. In the realm of relationships, for instance, many find themselves at an impasse, debating whether to express their feelings to someone they care about. Maria, a vibrant, creative soul, faced a paralyzing decision: confess her feelings to her close friend, Alex, or hold back and maintain the status quo.

Her fear loomed large, manifesting as two distinct voices. One voice cautioned her, advising caution and convincing her that friendship was a stable foundation. The other voice, a daring whisper, urged her to take the risk, highlighting the potential joy of mutual affection. Maria's journey through this emotional landscape illustrates the duality of fear; it can act as both a protective barrier and an exhilarating gateway to deeper connections.

As she navigated her feelings, she made it a practice to write her thoughts down, which unveiled not just the fears but also the hopes and dreams that flourished alongside them. Each page became a canvas where fear and possibility crafted a story of potential love. Eventually, Maria's fear transformed into a decision to embrace vulnerability; she confessed her feelings to Alex. Although initially fearful of rejection, she found that acknowledging her emotional companion—fear—allowed her to articulate her truth.

In this way, acknowledging fear not only empowers action

but also fosters heartfelt authenticity. Fear may whisper cautionary tales, but its presence can serve as a reminder that CHOICES rooted in love and honesty carry the deepest resonance with our truest selves.

Each anecdote of recognizing and acknowledging fear as a companion deepens our understanding of its role in the landscape of CHOICES. Yet, it is critical to articulate how to live alongside it—how to engage fear without allowing it to dominate our decisions. The trick lies in creating a partnership of sorts; rather than ignoring or suppressing fear's existence, we can learn to invite it along for the ride.

As we progress along the path of decision-making, let us examine the mechanics of this dance. What does it mean to engage with fear without being overwhelmed by it? It is in the practice of mindful awareness that the dance begins.

Mindfulness, a tool recognized by many spiritual traditions, invites us to observe our thoughts and feelings without attachment. When fear arises, instead of shying away from it, we can observe the sensations it brings and examine the truths it reveals about ourselves. Take time to pause, breathe deeply, and check in with our bodies.

For example, when facing an important presentation at

work, rather than succumbing to the urge to flee or overly fixate on worst-case scenarios, one can engage in a moment of stillness. Acknowledge the tightness in the chest and the racing heartbeat. Recognize these sensations as manifestations of fear, which exists to protect. Then, with grounded awareness, remind oneself of past successes, visualizing the exhilaration of those moments and the joy of sharing valuable insights with colleagues. This simple pause can recalibrate the experience of fear from overwhelming to manageable, allowing clarity to enter.

Moreover, the act of personifying fear can also reframe the relationship we have with it. When we view fear not as an enemy but rather as a companion, we begin to see it through a new lens. We can visualize fear as a character—a quirky friend who pipes up at the wrong moments, offering unsolicited advice. Instead of squashing that friend's presence, we can invite them to sit down beside us in the car as we drive toward our decision. This unique visualization allows for an exploration of fear as a part of our journey rather than an obstacle in our path.

So, how do we truly invite fear into the conversation? Share stories. Share laughter. When we find ourselves huddled under fear's shadow, taking the time to articulate its voice can create space for empowerment. For instance, Nicole, an artist, often found herself weighed down by the fear of judgment when pursuing her passion. But one day, after a particularly challenging critique session, she decided to voice this fear out loud. She gathered friends for a dinner filled with vulnerability where they exchanged stories about their own fears surrounding their pursuits.

Those conversations cultivated community and fostered connection. Each story served as a thread, weaving together a beautiful fabric of shared experiences. They weren't just articulating their fears; they were normalizing them, transforming fear from an isolating experience into a collective journey. Through this lens, fear transforms from a weighty burden into a shared experience that is acknowledged and understood by others.

As we engage with fear through shared storytelling, we can uncover layers of truth that might otherwise remain hidden. Each encounter with fear offers a lesson; it teaches us the value of resilience and the beauty of healing through community. We recognize how our paths intersect and how, together, we can find courage in the achingly familiar dance between hope and fear.

Fear often speaks in absolutes: "You will fail," "You aren't enough," "What will they think?" But amid the chaos, a whispered truth remains: "You have the power to choose." This recognition empowers us to confront fear directly, to redefine our narratives in the light of possibility. This empowers transformative CHOICES, places we never anticipated we could reach.

By cultivating a relationship with fear, we find that it becomes less domineering and more like a trustworthy friend. It can inform our decisions while still allowing us the room to stretch and grow. We begin to see the blend of intuition and intellect that exists within us—the two do not always have to be at odds. Instead, we can allow intuition to rise above the cacophony of fear, guiding us to CHOICES that ultimately reflect our authentic selves.

When we combine our intuition with the insights fear offers, we create a robust toolkit for navigating CHOICES. This toolkit encourages us to examine our motivations behind each decision: what truly lies behind our fears? By exploring our reactions, we can identify patterns and unravel the threads that bind us to outdated beliefs.

Some fear arises from societal conditioning, weighing down

our hearts with expectations of how we should act or what paths we should follow. Understanding this backdrop of conditioning empowers us to disentangle ourselves; it creates space for liberation. One may recognize cultural backgrounds, familial pressures, or other influences that have shaped their fears. By detangling these threads, we can make space for new narratives—those of empowerment and CHOICE.

Every story we share about fear is an opportunity to rewrite its meaning in our lives. Each experience brings with it lessons learned, perspectives gained, and an understanding that fear can often reveal the very essence of our growth. The next time fear makes its presence felt—when it tugs at your sleeve and tells you to hide—try to embrace that sensation. Acknowledge your feelings, share your stories, and dance with fear as your companion instead of your captor. Remind yourself that each step taken, each CHOICE made, moves you closer to a life of authenticity and fulfillment.

Empowered by the acknowledgment of fear, you can cultivate resilience—an unwavering spirit that propels you through uncertainties and trials. As you traverse the ever-evolving landscape of CHOICE, remember that fear may be your companion, but it does not define your journey. Each dance step you take alongside fear brings you closer to your ultimate destination: a life rich with intention and possibility, where each CHOICE shapes your unique narrative.

As we draw this exploration of fear as a companion to a close, we are reminded of the transformative power it can wield. All emotions, including fear, are part of the intricate tapestry of life. Fear can guide us; it can teach us; it can connect us. The more we understand and acknowledge it, the more we engage with our essence. As we learn to dance with fear—by acknowledging it, sharing it, and utilizing it as a guide—we unlock the power to reshape our CHOICES. It is through this relationship that we find courage and reveal our true selves, crafting a life illuminated by intention and growth.

Strategies to Tame Fear

Fear often lurks in the shadows of our minds, whispering doubts that keep us from pursuing our dreams. The dialogue in our heads can spiral into a cacophony that paralyzes us at times, yet it doesn't have to define our lives. The power to reshape our relationship with fear lies in our hands. In this subchapter, we will explore tangible strategies to confront and mitigate fear through practical steps that encompass mindfulness, breathing techniques, and affirmations. Each approach will empower readers to craft personalized methods to tackle trepidation and reclaim their sense of agency.

To begin this journey, let's first understand the role of fear. Fear is a natural emotional response that acts as a protective mechanism. It alerts us to potential dangers, prompting us to respond and adapt. However, when fear becomes overwhelming, it can restrict our opportunities and hinder growth. Therefore, the first step in taming fear is acknowledging its presence, understanding its roots, and recognizing that while fear is a universal experience, our responses can transform it into a catalyst for personal development.

Embracing Mindfulness

Mindfulness serves as a cornerstone in combating fear. It cultivates a heightened awareness of our thoughts and feelings, thus enabling us to observe our fears without judgment. By practicing mindfulness, we create a space where fear can be examined rather than reacted to.

1.   **Mindful Observation**: Start by setting aside a few minutes each day for mindful observation. Find a quiet space where you can sit comfortably. Close your eyes, take a deep breath, and focus your attention inward. As you breathe, notice any sensations in your body, the rise and fall of your chest, or

147

the warmth of the air entering and leaving your nostrils. When thoughts about your fears arise, acknowledge them—"I see you, fear"—and then gently redirect your focus back to your breath. This practice will help build a non-reactive stance toward fear, allowing you to respond thoughtfully rather than impulsively.

2. **Body Scan Meditation**: The body scan meditation is a wonderful tool to ground yourself and connect with the present moment. Lying down comfortably, begin at the top of your head and slowly move your attention down your body. With each breath, release tension or discomfort you may notice, particularly in areas where fear and anxiety manifest physically—perhaps in your chest, shoulders, or stomach. As you progress through your body, visualize fear dissolving with each exhale, leaving you lighter and more at ease.

3. **Mindfulness Journaling**: Maintain a mindfulness journal dedicated to your experiences with fear. Each day, set aside time to write down any fears you encountered and observe how they impacted your day. Focus on your feelings, where you felt fear physically, and how you reacted. By putting your fears to paper, you give them less power over you. Reflection will also reveal patterns in your fear responses, enabling you to address them more effectively.

Breathing Techniques

Breath is an immediate conduit to our state of mind. Techniques that emphasize breathing can significantly reduce the physiological and psychological effects of fear. Let's explore some effective methods:

1. **Deep Breathing**: In moments of anxiety, your breath often becomes shallow. Take time to engage in deep breathing. Inhale deeply through your nose, allowing your abdomen to expand fully; then slowly exhale through your mouth. Aim for a count of four on the inhale, hold for a count of four, and exhale for a count of six. This method activates your parasympathetic nervous system, helping to calm your body and mind.

2. **Box Breathing**: This is a powerful technique used by those in high-pressure situations, including athletes and military personnel. Visualize a box as you breathe: inhale for a count of four while mentally tracing one side of the box, hold for four, exhale for four while tracing the second side down, and hold again for four before starting the next cycle. Repeat this process several times until you feel a noticeable shift in your body's tension levels.

3. **5-4-3-2-1 Method**: This grounding technique uses

breath alongside sensory engagement. Begin by taking a deep breath, and then name five things you can see, four things you can touch, three things you can hear, two things you can smell, and one thing you can taste. This exercise reconnects you to your physical environment, distracting the brain from fear.

Affirmations for Empowerment

The language we use shapes our thoughts, and powerful affirmations can counteract fear's negative whispers. Affirmations are positive statements that can uplift and fortify your sense of self. Start incorporating them into your daily routine:

1. **Creating Personalized Affirmations**: Write down affirmations that resonate with you personally. Consider specific fears you want to address. For example, if you fear failure, your affirmation might be: "I learn and grow through every experience, and I embrace failure as a stepping stone to success." Repeat these affirmations aloud every morning when you wake up and every night before you sleep. Over time, consistent repetition will shift your belief patterns.

2. **Visualization**: Pair affirmations with visualization techniques. Close your eyes and envision yourself in a situation where you typically feel fear. As you picture it, repeat your

affirmation, feeling its energy imbue your vision. Visualize success in overcoming the fear, reinforcing the powerful connection between thought, emotion, and outcome.

3.   **Affirmation Cards**: Create affirmation cards with your written statements, decorating them to reflect your personality. Place them where you'll see them often—on your bathroom mirror, car dashboard, or workspace. The constant reminder will serve as a reassuring presence, encouraging you to embrace and confront fear when it surfaces.

Establishing a Routine

Building a routine around these practices will cement them into your life, allowing you to face fear with resilience. Create a daily schedule that includes time for mindfulness, breathing exercises, and affirmations.

1.   **Morning Ritual**: Begin each day with a morning ritual that consists of a brief mindfulness observation, deep breathing, and affirmations. This process sets a positive tone for your day, establishing a mindset that is proactive rather than reactive.

2.   **Mindful Check-ins**: Throughout your day, designate specific moments for quick check-ins. This can be as simple as

a minute spent focusing on your breath or reminding yourself of an affirmation. Use these moments to recalibrate, especially when you feel anxiety creeping back in.

3. **Evening Reflection**: Conclude each day with an evening reflection. Acknowledge your fears, what you faced successfully, and where you struggled. Affirm your strength in dealing with challenges and commit to using the tools discussed here in the future. Writing these reflections can strengthen the neural pathways that enhance resilience against fear.

Seeking Support

Overcoming fear is a journey best undertaken not in isolation but in community. Sharing anxieties can lessen their hold over you and facilitate growth through mutual support. Consider the following options:

1. **Finding a Mindfulness Buddy**: Connect with someone who shares your desire for self-improvement. Schedule regular meet-ups or virtual sessions to practice mindfulness and breathing exercises together. This collective experience can motivate both parties and create a safe space for vulnerability.

2. **Join a Support Group**: Many communities offer support groups focused on anxiety and fear. Engaging with others who share similar struggles can be immensely therapeutic. Listening to others' journeys and sharing your own fosters a sense of connection, reinforcing that fear does not need to be faced alone.

3. **Professional Guidance**: When fear feels insurmountable, consider seeking guidance from a therapist or counselor. Professionals trained to handle anxiety can provide specialized tools and coping strategies tailored to your specific needs, offering a robust foundation for overcoming fear.

Embracing Courage

While the strategies above equip you with tools to manage fear, they also promote the cultivation of courage. Courage is not the absence of fear; it is the determination to act in spite of it. Embrace small challenges that push your boundaries.

1. **Start Small**: Implement the strategies gradually. Begin by facing minor fears or anxieties and gradually work your way up to larger challenges. Celebrate each success, no matter how small, as it serves to reinforce courage within.

2. **Document Your Journey**: Keep a journal dedicated

to your experiences with fear and courage. Record when you faced a fear, how you felt, and the outcome. This allows you to see your progress over time, reinforcing your ability to confront fear.

3. **Create a Courage Mantra**: Alongside your affirmations, develop a courage mantra to keep at the forefront of your mind. This could be as simple as, "I choose to face my fears. I am capable. I am strong." Use it during moments of doubt to remind yourself of your inner strength.

Practicing Self-Compassion

Finally, be gentle with yourself through this process. Fear is a deeply rooted emotion, and the journey to navigate it is not linear. Acknowledge days when fear feels stronger and be compassionate with yourself during those times. The goal is not to eradicate fear but to create a healthy relationship with it.

In summary, the strategies presented in this subchapter provide a robust framework for confronting fear and transforming it into an ally rather than an adversary. By integrating mindfulness, breathing techniques, and affirmations into your daily routine, you create pathways toward a life marked by agency rather than fear. As you embrace these practices, remember that each small step taken is part of a larger journey of growth and self-discovery. The dance with fear may continue, but with courage and intention, you can lead that dance with grace.

The Dance of Courage

Fear. It's a word that can strike a chord in anyone, sending shivers down the spine or causing the stomach to twist in knots. For many, fear is viewed as a hindrance, an obstacle that prevents them from pursuing their dreams or living life to the fullest. However, what if this very sensation we dread could serve as a dynamic companion, guiding us toward growth and self-discovery? This chapter, "The Dance of Courage," invites you to reconsider fear's role in your life and to explore the artistry of engaging with it in a way that transforms it from an adversary into a partner.

Imagine, if you will, a dance floor—a vast expanse where possibilities unfold, and the music of life plays. In this setting, fear enters like an unexpected partner. At first, you may be hesitant, unsure of how to engage with this entity that often feels overwhelming and constricting. However, as the music swells and the rhythm takes hold, you come to recognize that fear, like a partner in dance, has a role to play. It can lead you to explore new movements, challenge your boundaries, and discover hidden depths of resilience within you.

As you step onto this metaphorical dance floor, envision fear extending its hand, inviting you to join it in this intricate choreography of life. At first, you might fumble, your steps unsure as you navigate the complexities of this unusual partnership. But over time, and with practice, you begin to recognize the beauty in these movements—how they push you beyond your comfort zone, coaxing forth courage and enabling you to twirl joyfully into the unknown.

Consider the story of Amelia, a woman who spent years locked in a job that drained her spirit. Amelia had always dreamed of being a painter, losing herself in vibrant colors and imaginative landscapes. However, fear whispered incessantly in her ear: "What if you fail? What if no one likes your art? What if you can't make it?" These fears held her back until one day, a friend invited her to an art exhibit. As Amelia walked through the gallery, she felt a stirring within her—a longing to express herself through her own painting.

That evening, Amelia went home, heart racing, but exhilarated by the possibility of creation. She picked up her brush, dipped it into bold hues, and allowed fear to dance alongside her. Instead of shying away from her doubts, she invited them into her creative process. With every stroke, Amelia confronted the insecurities that had plagued her for so long. Each canvas she painted became an intimate dialogue with fear—a fusion of vulnerability and expression.

As she embraced her fears, Amelia found herself not only producing art but thriving in a profound way. Participation in local art shows followed, and to her surprise, the validation she sought from others came—yet it felt secondary to the empowerment she discovered within herself. Her dance with fear had transformed her; it became a source of inspiration rather than a roadblock.

Now, let's take a moment to consider your own dance with fear. Grab a journal or find a quiet space to reflect. As you prepare to document your journey, here are some prompts to guide your exploration:

1. **Identify Your Fear**: What specific fears have you encountered in your life? Write them down in detail. How have they held you back?

2. **Acknowledge Your Feelings**: When that fear arises, what emotions come up for you? Are there physical sensations associated with fear—tightness in your chest, a racing heart, or a sense of dread?

3. **Confronting Fear**: Describe a time when you faced one of these fears. What was the outcome? How did it change your relationship with that fear?

4. **Inviting Fear to Dance**: How can you invite this fear into your life? What practical steps can you take to engage with it rather than running away?

5. **The Celebration**: After you confront your fear, how do you feel? Write about the growth and empowerment that comes from dancing with it.

As you document your journey, remember that each step you take is an affirmation that allows fear to be part of the experience, rather than an isolated threat. Consider also the stories of those who have engaged with their fears and emerged triumphantly.

Another powerful narrative is that of James, a man who had long battled with social anxiety. For years, he avoided gatherings, fearing judgment and ridicule. He would grapple with negative self-talk as he stood at the threshold of any social event, grappling with thoughts of being misunderstood.

One day, determined to shift his experience, James decided to sign up for a dance class. The initial sessions were excruciating; his body stiffened with apprehension, and his mind buzzed with anxiety. However, rather than allowing that fear to paralyze him, James forced himself to engage. The dance floor became his field of battle, where he challenged himself to step beyond the confines of his comfort zone.

With each lesson, James gradually found his footing, allowing fear to teach him the rhythm of connection. He started to talk to fellow dancers, sharing laughter and mutual awkwardness. The fears that had once controlled him began to wane, replaced by an invigorating sense of belonging.

Through the dance of shared vulnerability, James discovered the paradox of engaging with his fear: the more he leaned into it, the more freedom he began to experience. His social anxiety, once an impenetrable wall, transformed into an opportunity for interpersonal connection.

As you ponder these stories, consider how fear can become a conduit for community and connection. Fear shouldn't isolate us; rather, it can bring us together in shared experiences, where we realize that we are not alone. Engaging with fear becomes a communal dance, allowing for opportunity and growth.

The next reflective prompt to engage with your dance includes:

6.   **Connecting with Others**: How has fear manifested in your relationships? Have there been moments where shared vulnerability has strengthened your connections?

7.   **Find Your Community**: What spaces can you move into that encourage discussion and connection around fears?

8.   **Support Systems**: Who can you turn to for support in facing your fears? Write about this network that motivates you to engage courageously.

9.   **Celebrating Your Growth**: Write about moments of triumph where you danced with fear in community contexts. How did these experiences shape your interactions with others?

Through these reflective exercises, you will find a nuanced relationship with fear—acknowledging that embracing it fosters growth not only within ourselves but in the broader tapestry of life.

As we continue this exploration, consider the metaphor of the dance itself. A good dance is not just about precision; it's about the fluidity of movement, the ability to adapt, change directions, and sometimes even stumble. In the same way, when we dance with fear, it is crucial to remember that overcoming fear does not imply perfection.

Defining courage in the dance of life is about remembering that stumbles and hesitations can be part of the experience. Dancing defiantly does not mean a lack of fear; it means choosing to move regardless.

Let's revisit Amelia and James. Both created art and connections, not because they were fearless, but because they chose to don their dancing shoes and step out onto the floor. Their narratives are infused with the reality of vulnerability yet highlight an unwavering love for the dance.

Reflect on your own narrative—what have you learned from your missteps? Here is another series of prompts to assist you on this path:

10. **Embracing Mistakes**: What mistakes have you made when dancing through your fears? How have they contributed to your understanding of courage?

11. **The Lessons of Vulnerability**: In what ways have your mistakes led to unexpected outcomes or lessons?

12. **The Beauty of Imperfection**: How can embracing imperfection enhance your experience of living? Write about situations where imperfection became a source of growth.

As you navigate these reflections, it's imperative to remember: courage is not a paintbrush used to erase fear;

161

instead, it is an instrument that acknowledges fear's presence and still dares to dance amidst it.

As we reach the climax of this chapter, let us engage with one final story, that of Maya—an aspiring writer whose passion for words was overshadowed by fear of rejection. Having birthed countless drafts, she battled with insecurity as she sent her heartfelt stories out into the world.

Maya learned to partner with her fear of judgment, to let it guide her but not define her. When she received feedback (both positive and critical), she began to treat each response as encouragement to refine her dance. Each critique was a mirror reflecting areas for growth, essential in her journey as an artist. Instead of withdrawing, she chose to celebrate each opportunity to engage, recognizing that every interaction enriched her writing.

The tips Maya picked up along the way added layers to her writing process. Similar to a dance routine flush with choreography, her storytelling evolved, increasingly cohesive and vibrant with every revision. As fear transformed into an ally, Maya's stories gained depth, allowing her to express herself freely and authentically.

In developing your courage and forging a dance with fear,

use the following prompts to fuse your reflections into actionable insights:

13. **Continuous Evolution**: How do you see your relationship with fear evolving over time?

14. **Honoring Your Journey**: As you move forward, how can you honor both your fears and your accomplishments?

15. **Cultivating a Dance Rhythm**: Identify rhythms or practices that allow you to continually engage with fear in a way that nurtures your growth.

Harness these reflections, let your journey unfold, and invite fear to serve as a dance partner in the ongoing saga of your life. Each sway, each pivot, embodies the courage that resides deep within you, waiting to be expressed.

Fear does not disappear, nor should it. Rather, dance with it. Embrace its presence. The next time it calls you to the floor, respond with grace, vulnerability, and a willingness to embrace the exhilarating possibilities that arise when we dare to dance with our fears.

Choosing Love over Fear

The Power of Love

In the grand tapestry of human experience, few threads shine as brightly as love. Love is a force that shapes destinies, inspires growth, and fosters connections that elevate the human spirit beyond the mundane confines of existence. It acts as both a guiding light and a sanctuary, beckoning us to Choose paths suffused with warmth and compassion rather than fear and hesitation.

Throughout history, countless stories have emerged that

encapsulate the transformative power of love. These narratives, rooted in fervent emotions and profound revelations, serve as reminders of what is possible when we open ourselves to this boundless force. As we delve into the essence of love, we begin to uncover the depths of its ability to nurture personal growth and cultivate fulfilling relationships.

To truly appreciate the power of love, one must first grasp its inherent qualities. Love is not merely an emotion; it is a CHOICE, a commitment embedded in the very fabric of our interactions with others and ourselves. Each decision to act with love is an affirmation of our values, a reflection of who we are, and a reminder of our capacity to forge connections that transcend superficial barriers.

Consider the story of Sarah and David, who exemplify the transformative journey love can inspire. Sarah was a talented artist, yet for years, she fought against a paralyzing fear of inadequacy. Ever since childhood, she was taught to measure her worth by her accomplishments, leaving little room for self-love and acceptance. This fear created a self-imposed barrier between her passions and her potential. Despite her artistic talents, she found herself in a stagnant job, afraid to take the leap into the creative world where her heart truly lay.

Then, David entered her life. A gentle soul radiating kindness, David saw beyond Sarah's insecurities. He loved her not only for her artistry but for her dreams and aspirations. His belief in her rekindled the flickering flame within Sarah. Encouraged by his unwavering support, she began to explore her artistic abilities more fully. It was through love that Sarah discovered the courage to embrace her true self—an act that catalyzed profound growth.

As Sarah delved deeper into her art, she became increasingly aware of the healing properties intertwined in the creative process. With each brushstroke, she poured her emotions onto the canvas, shedding layers of self-doubt and fostering self-acceptance. It was as if the love she received from David permeated her creations, transforming her work into a celebration of resilience and beauty.

Their relationship flourished through mutual support and encouragement, with David pursuing his passion for music alongside Sarah's artistic journey. This shared devotion fostered a unique bond that reinforced their individual growth. Instead of allowing the fear of failure to dictate the course of their lives, they Chose love as the guiding principle.

The love between Sarah and David not only enriched their

lives but also inspired their families and friends. Witnessing their unwavering connection, those around them began to re-evaluate their own relationships—both romantic and platonic. The ripple effect of love spread beyond their immediate surroundings, catalyzing change in others and nurturing an environment of positivity and understanding.

In this way, love acts as a transformative energy that extends beyond personal boundaries. It is a thread that weaves through communities, connecting individuals who might otherwise remain islands of isolation. Each person touched by love can become a vessel for its essence, igniting compassion within others. This interconnectedness underscores the profound importance of Choosing love over fear in our daily lives.

Perhaps one of the most poignant examples of love's transformative nature can be found in the tales of parents and their children. The bond formed between a parent and child serves as a powerful testament to the significance of love as a guiding CHOICE. When parents lean into love—nurturing their children's potential rather than succumbing to fears of failure—they cultivate an atmosphere rich with growth, exploration, and self-discovery.

Take, for instance, a father named Michael who faced

societal pressure to mold his son, Alex, into a reflection of himself—one of conformity and success. Initially motivated by a desire to see Alex become a career-driven individual like himself, Michael imposed rigid expectations on his son. However, as Michael's heart grew in love for Alex, an awakening occurred. He realized that true strength lay in celebrating Alex's unique interests, even if they diverged from traditional definitions of success. The shift from fear of societal judgment to love for his son's individuality empowered Michael to let go of preconceived notions.

By embracing a love that allowed Alex to flourish in his authentic self, Michael created a nurturing environment where creativity, confidence, and a sense of identity could take root. Alex developed his love for science, exploring curiosity without the weight of fear that often accompanies parental expectations. As they each Chose love, an unparalleled bond blossomed—one that strengthened as they learned from one another.

Navigating the complexities of love also calls for vulnerability. To love deeply is to expose oneself to the possibility of pain, disappointment, and heartbreak. Yet, it is within this vulnerability that we often find the purity and strength of love. The willingness to be open and honest in our relationships invites authentic connections, allowing us to discover layers of intimacy not typically accessible in fear-laden encounters.

Jessica and Tom's relationship illustrates this beautifully. Both came into their partnership with scars from past relationships—fearful of repeating painful patterns. Initially, they navigated their connection with trepidation, struggling with trust and vulnerability. However, through shared experiences and open communication, they began to dismantle the walls surrounding their hearts. Choosing love meant confronting their fears head-on, rather than allowing them to dictate the dynamic of their relationship.

Through genuine conversations and moments of shared laughter, Jessica and Tom fostered a sense of safety that encouraged mutual vulnerability. They articulated their fears, desires, and visions for the future, allowing each other the space to grow. This commitment to love, even when fear loomed large, transformed their connection into a profound exploration of shared dreams and aspirations.

The lessons learned through their relationship rippled into other aspects of their lives, transforming friendships and family dynamics alike. As Jessica and Tom dismantled their walls, they inspired those around them to reflect on their own relationships, fostering a more collective culture of vulnerability rooted in love.

In realizing that love can encompass both joy and pain, we come to understand that the transformative quality of love is often born through struggles. While fear tempts us to avoid discomfort, love urges us to embrace it. By Choosing love, we cultivate resilience, fortitude, and an unwavering commitment to growth.

The stories of Sarah, Michael, Jessica, and Tom exemplify the power of love in navigating challenges and embracing connections that enrich our lives. Yet, it is essential to acknowledge that love is not a panacea; it does not negate the presence of fear. Instead, love empowers individuals to confront those fears and transform them, creating spaces where growth can unfold.

Cultivating a mindset centered on love involves awareness of the CHOICES we make daily. Each moment presents an opportunity for love to manifest—be it through kindness in our interactions, support for a friend in need, or sharing moments of joy with loved ones. These seemingly small CHOICES culminate in significant impacts, reinforcing the essence of love as a powerful guiding force.

As we navigate life's challenges, we can consciously Choose to infuse every encounter with love. Simple gestures—an encouraging word, a grateful heart, a listening ear—act as catalysts for connection, opening paths that foster deeper relationships. When we love intentionally, we allow ourselves to grow alongside those we care about, transforming not only our lives but also the world around us.

Let us not forget the transformative potential of self-love in this journey. The foundation of loving others truly begins with nurturing our relationship with ourselves. By embracing our imperfections and honoring our worth, we empower ourselves to extend love toward those around us. Self-love is not selfish; it is essential in cultivating a depth of compassion that can overflow into our relationships with others.

Through the lens of self-love, every CHOICE we make becomes an act of love manifested outwardly. When we Choose to be kind to ourselves, to set boundaries that honor our needs, and to celebrate our unique journey, we create a space for love to flourish. This internal transformation not only nurtures our personal growth but also enhances the quality of our relationships, allowing others to witness and reciprocate that love.

Choosing love also invites the possibility of healing, both for ourselves and for those around us. Love acts as a salve for wounds that, if left unattended, fester and impede our growth. It encourages us to confront grievances and misunderstandings, fostering an environment where reconciliation and understanding can thrive.

For example, consider the story of Emma and Liam, who found themselves drifting apart as unresolved conflicts loomed over their relationship. The fear of addressing contentious issues led to the gradual deterioration of their bond, leaving both feeling isolated and unheard. It was not until an unexpected conversation sparked by an act of kindness that the couple dared to confront their fears together. Choosing love became an act of vulnerability—an opportunity to address grievances openly and honestly.

Through sharing their feelings and experiences, Emma and Liam embarked on a healing journey that transformed their relationship. Rather than allowing fear to dictate their interactions, they embraced the power of love to foster understanding. This CHOICE not only mended their bond but also reinforced their belief in the potential of love to heal and nurture.

The journey toward cultivation and celebration of love is ongoing, often requiring introspection, reflection, and commitment. It challenges us to confront our fears, nurture our relationships with patience, and practice gratitude for the abundance love brings.

The simple act of expressing gratitude can be a profound reminder of love's presence in our lives. By appreciating the small yet significant moments of love, we create a culture grounded in thankfulness, further reinforcing our connections.

In their exploration of gratitude, the stories of many individuals reveal that love unfurling in their lives often bears fruit through a deeper appreciation. One such story involves siblings Lily and Ben, who grew increasingly distant as adulthood pulled them in different directions. However, through shared memories and expressions of gratitude for one another, they rekindled their bond.

Lily discovered the value of love's presence in her life as she took the time to appreciate her brother's steadfast support throughout their childhood. Writing Ben a heartfelt letter of gratitude transformed their relationship, fostering a new sense of understanding and appreciation that bridged the distance.

In traveling through these narratives, we uncover a universal truth: the CHOICES we make in love can forge connections, foster healing, inspire growth, and create legacies that transcend both time and space. It is through Choosing love that we invite the possibility of transformation in our lives and, ultimately, in the world around us.

As we reflect on our journeys, let us consider how love has played a transformative role in our lives. What loving decisions have shaped the course of your existence? How has Choosing love changed your identity, aspirations, and relationships?

In allowing ourselves to dwell in these reflections, we cultivate an appreciation that strengthens our resolve to Choose love over fear in the face of life's uncertainties. We find courage in stories shared, embrace vulnerability as a source of strength, and honor the power of love as a guiding CHOICE. By practicing love in our daily lives, we carve pathways filled with compassion, growth, and, ultimately, the richness of connection.

Choosing love promises the potential for discovery, joy, and fulfillment, reminding us that the journey toward profound transformation begins with the heart. Through love, we reveal new dimensions of ourselves, uniting us in a shared narrative that continues to evolve, inspire, and illuminate the possibilities available to us all.

The Intersection of Hope

In the delicate weave of our lives, moments arise that challenge our perception, pulling us between the powerful forces of love and fear. These pivotal moments, often silent yet thunderous, cast long shadows over our CHOICES, urging us to either retreat into the comfort of despair or step boldly into the light of hope. It is within this interplay that we discover the transformative power of love, standing as both a beacon and a guide, illuminating our paths even when fear threatens to dim our resolve.

The first breath of awareness often comes with a confluence of emotions, but it is the capacity to love that truly shapes the tapestry of our CHOICES. Those who have walked through the valley of fear know the weight it bears—an invisible cloak that wraps around the heart, squeezing tight with anxiety and uncertainty. Yet beyond that veil lies love, a force so immense and pure it has the power to dismantle heavily woven fears and replace them with hope.

Consider Sarah, a single mother who faced the crossroads of her life when her partner left unexpectedly. The initial shock of betrayal loomed over her like a storm cloud, each drop of rain a reminder of her loss, her fear of raising her child alone, and her overwhelming sense of inadequacy. In that moment, despair became a familiar companion, whispering words of defeat into her ear. It was easy to listen—to let the emotions wash over her like a tidal wave, pulling her under and making her question her worth. But, in an unexpected turn, it was the love for her child that sparked a glimmer of hope.

Every night, as she tucked her son into bed, she would look into his eyes and realize that her fear was not just her own. It was a shadow she was casting over his bright, hopeful spirit. In those moments of vulnerability, she Chose love. She did not know how she would navigate the impending obstacles—financial instability, the stigma of being a single parent, or her own feelings of unworthiness. Nonetheless, the CHOICE to engage in love for her child transformed her despair into determination.

"Hope is the thing with feathers," Emily Dickinson wrote. These moments where we Choose love allow hope to take flight, spreading its wings and guiding us through the darkest storms. For Sarah, it meant getting up every day and giving her best, not just for herself but for the little boy who depended on her. She began to see the beauty around her, even in the chaos—small moments, like laughter shared over breakfast and bedtime stories. Love, in her case, became a catalyst for change—an invitation to step beyond her trauma and embrace a reality built on resilience.

When we Choose hope, we do not ignore fear; instead, we acknowledge it as a part of our human experience. Sarah didn't magically forget her struggles. They remained present, albeit with a different narrative. Each time fear reared its head, she responded not with capitulation but with a commitment to love—to her son, to herself, and to the possibilities that lay ahead. This CHOICE gave her strength.

The act of Choosing love over fear gives us permission to embrace our authentic selves. In moments of despair, it often becomes essential to engage in self-acceptance. The journey through turmoil can be riddled with self-doubt, but it is crucial to recognize that feelings are valid, and fears do not define us. Every individual who has faced fear has an opportunity for growth, a chance to shed old skin and step into a powerful narrative of hope and healing.

Let us reflect on John, who faced a daunting diagnosis of cancer. The news struck like a lightning bolt, shattering the illusion of security and prompting immediate fears about life, death, and everything in between. Initially, the darkness was suffocating, encasing him in uncertainty. He found himself at the threshold of fear, trapped in the whirlwind of despair. It would have been easy to succumb, to let go of the joy and love surrounding him in life.

But amidst that haze of stark reality, a series of moments emerged—love from his family and friends, fiery and unyielding, beckoned him to Choose hope. During his treatments, instead of allowing the white walls of the hospital to stifle his spirit, John began documenting his journey through art. The brushstrokes on canvas became an expression of love, channeling his pain into profound imagery that depicted not only his struggles but also the unwavering hope he harbored in his heart. Each canvas was a testament to the love that surrounded him, echoing the voices of encouragement that whispered through the shadows of fear.

In those days, John learned that hope isn't merely the absence of fear; it is the assertive acknowledgment of love's presence, even in the face of uncertainty. The community that rallied around him shone like a lighthouse through foggy nights, guiding him toward brighter shores. They reminded him that Choosing hope and love is an act of bravery, not of avoidance.

Self-acceptance became an integral part of John's healing journey, as he learned to forgive himself for moments of weakness. He engaged in contemplative practices that allowed him to sit with his fear rather than running from it. By accepting every element of his experience, he could draw strength from it, transforming pain into empowerment—a powerful shift that propelled him toward acceptance.

These narratives of Sarah and John shine a light on the intricate connections between love and hope, illustrating how pivotal moments can redefine our CHOICES. They elucidate the heart of the matter, showing us not just how to confront fear, but how to surround it with love. It is love that forms the fabric of hope, sewing together the patches of despair into a quilt that is uniquely ours. When faced with fear, we must remember—we have a CHOICE.

As readers, we are encouraged to reflect on our own lives. What are the fears that loom on the horizon? Are there fears that have prevented us from reaching for love? Consider the moments that have challenged you. Were there decisions informed by love, leading you toward the light, even when fear threatened to overshadow your path? Embracing these reflections is the first step toward recognizing the immeasurable strength of hope. It exists within each of us, waiting to be summoned.

Engaging in self-acceptance means recognizing that our fears do not diminish us. They are experiences we can learn from and, ultimately, transform. When we acknowledge our vulnerabilities, we also allow ourselves the freedom to love fiercely and hope deeply. The act of Choosing love over fear is not presented as simplistic but as a courageous dialogue between self-compassion and the authentic expression of feelings.

An exercise to embody this principle might include a journal entry devoted to love and hope: Write down instances where love has emerged in challenging times and the CHOICES it inspired. Close your eyes and visualize each scenario—every CHOICE filled with intention and purpose. Let the validation of your experience wash over you. Each CHOICE made in love is a step toward growth, a badge of resilience that affirms your journey.

As we challenge ourselves to live amidst the confluence of love and fear, we must foster a mindset grounded in gratitude. Count the moments that fuel your hope; it could be a smile shared with a stranger or an unexpected gesture of kindness. Gratitude, like love, has the capacity to transcend fear, creating ripples of connection. Carla, a cancer survivor, experienced this firsthand when she circled back to the hospital that once felt like a prison of her illness. Instead of dwelling on the fears of her past, she Chose to share her story of recovery with newly diagnosed patients—transforming her fear into a fountain of hope for others. Her vulnerability and compassion built bridges where once there were walls.

Life has a way of inviting us to witness hope even when the world feels heavy. Choosing love enables us to challenge despair while allowing empathy to flourish. Our collective experiences illuminate the brilliance that hope can bring, spreading like wildfire through unexpected avenues. We need only look inward and find acceptance, nurturing the love that resides within ourselves and extends outward.

As we conclude this chapter, it is vital to recognize the ongoing dance between love and fear throughout our lives; it is not a singular event but a narrative that unfolds in layers, inviting us to embrace our humanity. Each story tells of trials faced and CHOICES made—a rich tapestry where love serves as both anchor and sail, propelling us through tumultuous waters. Choosing love over fear marks the journey toward healing and self-acceptance, a sweet reminder that, even amid turmoil, we can navigate the depths with confidence.

Engage with the lessons within you, breathe in courage, and allow yourself to envision the life you want to lead. Each step into love is a beacon of hope—rebirth in the face of adversity. Make the CHOICE today to embody hope, elevate love, and exchange fear for the beauty of connection with yourself and those around you. The path may not always be easy, yet it is filled with opportunities to grow and to love, not in the absence of fear, but resolutely in its face.

A Call to Action

In the grand tapestry of life, love stands as the thread that binds us to each other and to ourselves. It carries the potential to transform the mundane into the extraordinary and to uplift us in our darkest hours. As we begin to recognize the potency of our CHOICES, it becomes clear that prioritizing love over fear is not just a noble aspiration but a profound necessity. This realization compels us to take action, shifting our focus from the anxieties that often cloud our vision to the brighter, more hopeful possibilities that love enables.

This subchapter, "A Call to Action," serves as an invitation—a gentle nudge to step into a space of conscientious decision-making, where love is both the compass and the destination. We will explore actionable steps that place love at the forefront of our CHOICES, encouraging us to craft a personal action plan that resonates with our unique journeys.

Creating Your Action Plan

With the understanding that love can guide us, let's set the stage for our action plans. An effective action plan can be likened to a road map, guiding our way as we navigate the landscapes of our lives. It helps us identify where we stand, where we wish to go, and the steps necessary to reach our destinations.

Start by taking a moment to reflect on what love means to you. Is it kindness, compassion, or understanding? Is it expressed in grand gestures or in small, daily acts? Understanding what love signifies in your life is crucial before diving into the practical aspects of your action plan.

Grab a journal or a piece of paper. Allow yourself the freedom to explore your thoughts as we take the first steps toward creating an action plan that embodies love.

1. List Love-Based Decisions

Begin by writing down specific love-based decisions you can prioritize moving forward. These decisions can range from simple, everyday actions to more significant commitments that require deeper reflection and planning.

- **Everyday Acts of Love:** Consider how you can express love in your daily life. This might include acts of kindness toward strangers, compliments to friends, or dedicating time to loved ones. Jot them down.

- **Developing Emotional Intimacy:** Reflect on your closer relationships and write down ways to nurture emotional connection. This might involve scheduling regular check-ins with loved ones or sharing your feelings more openly.

- **Kindness to Yourself:** Don't forget to include decisions that foster love for yourself! List actions that affirm your self-worth and happiness, whether it's pursuing hobbies you enjoy, treating yourself with care, or setting healthy boundaries.

- **Support for Others:** Think about ways you can be a source of support for those around you. This could involve mentoring, volunteering, or simply being present when someone is struggling.

The goal is to paint a vivid picture of how love can manifest in your life, to steer your CHOICES toward actions that feed your spirit and those of others.

2. Set Specific Goals

Once you have your list, it's time to set achievable goals based on your love-based decisions. This step is essential as it converts aspirational thoughts into tangible commitments.

Be specific about your goals. Instead of stating, "I will be more loving," specify, "I will send one message of appreciation to a friend every week" or "I will spend every Sunday afternoon with my family to strengthen our bond."

Transforming vague intentions into actionable goals reinforces your commitment to moving forward with love as your focus. Write each goal beneath the corresponding decision in your action plan.

3. Identify Potential Obstacles

As you embark on this path, it's vital to acknowledge potential obstacles that may arise. Fear often creeps in when we commit to love, presenting doubts that may hinder our progress.

Take a moment to reflect on what might hold you back from embodying your love-based decisions. Are there fears of vulnerability or of being let down? Do your past experiences loom large in your psyche, casting shadows over new commitments? Write these obstacles down, and prepare to face them head-on.

4. Develop Strategies to Overcome Challenges

Identify the fears and barriers from the previous step as areas of focus, then brainstorm strategies to confront these challenges. This proactive approach will allow you to navigate potential pitfalls with grace and resilience.

For instance:

- If you worry about vulnerability, can you practice opening up in small doses first?

- If time constraints seem overwhelming, can you designate specific periods each week solely for love-based interactions?

- Consider reaching out to supportive friends who can offer encouragement when you feel unsure.

Write down the strategies next to the respective obstacles, creating a roadmap that maps out not just where you want to go but also how to surmount any bumps along the way.

5. Accountability

Next, consider establishing accountability to support your

journey. Community fosters growth, providing the encouragement we need during challenging times.

Can you partner with a friend or family member who shares similar goals? You might agree to check in with each other regularly about your actions and progress, encouraging and inspiring one another to stay committed to a loving path.

You could also consider joining groups, whether they are local or online, that focus on personal growth or love-centric initiatives. Sharing your action plan with trusted individuals and asking for their support instills a sense of responsibility to engage actively in your commitment.

6. Celebrate Progress and Adjust

As you embark on this adventure, celebrate every small victory. Acknowledging progress, no matter the size, fuels motivation and reinforces your commitment to love. Create small rituals for celebrating your milestones, whether it's treating yourself to a favorite meal or sharing your achievements with friends.

Be willing to revisit and adjust your action plan as needed. Recognition and growth are dynamic processes that require reevaluation and flexibility. If, for instance, an approach isn't bringing the desired effect, don't hesitate to modify your strategies or goals. Embrace the fluidity of growth: it is a natural part of your journey.

Incorporating Love into the Everyday

Loving actions can also be incorporated into various aspects of your everyday life, making love an inseparable part of your routine. When love informs our daily CHOICES, it becomes a lens through which we view the world.

- **Mindfulness Practices:** Start each day with a moment of gratitude. Reflect on the aspects of your life filled with love, whether they are relationships, opportunities, or personal attributes you cherish.

- **Acts of Service:** Find ways to serve others in your community. This could mean volunteering with a local charity, helping a neighbor, or offering support to a friend in need.

- **Quality Time:** Prioritize quality time with loved ones by scheduling regular outings or catch-up phone calls. Use this time to foster deeper connections and understanding.

- **Affirmations of Love:** Use positive

affirmations to boost your mindset. Each morning, deliver affirmations focusing on love—whether directed toward yourself or others—to set a compassionate tone for the day.

- **The Language of Love:** Learn about love languages, both your own and those of the people in your life. Understanding how you and others express and receive love can provide profound insights into creating deeper connections.

Inviting Transformation

As you craft your action plan to prioritize love, you step into a transformative space. This action plan is not just a collection of intentions; it is a powerful commitment to live with intention and purpose. As you consciously Choose love over fear, the world around you will begin to reflect these decisions.

You will find that the love you embody not only enriches your life but ripples outward, affecting those you interact with and even the broader community. Each loving decision creates a wave of positivity, potentially inspiring others to make similar CHOICES.

Conclusion: A Shift in Narrative

In conclusion, this call to action is an invitation to alter your life narrative. Prioritizing love is an opportunity to align your CHOICES with your core values and desires, leading to a more fulfilled existence.

Through crafting a personalized action plan, you build a framework that empowers you to consciously Choose love amid life's complexities. This journey requires courage—a leap of faith toward embracing vulnerability and connection.

As you embark on this journey of prioritizing love in your life, remember that it is a continuous process. Every CHOICE you make, every connection you foster, and every statement of love will contribute to the legacy you create—not just for yourself, but for those who come after you. Embrace this journey with an open heart, reflecting on the transformative potential that love offers.

The CHOICE is yours. Let love guide you forward.

The CHOICE to Change

Embracing Transformation

The journey of life is a constant ebb and flow of growth, shaped by the CHOICES we make. Each decision becomes a thread woven into the intricate fabric of our existence, creating a tapestry that depicts who we are and who we aspire to become. Transformation often requires us to confront our fears and embrace the vulnerability that comes with stepping outside our comfort zones. In this exploration, we delve into the profound impact of CHOICE on personal transformation, drawing upon the stories of both The Seeker and The Mentor. Each story unfolds as a testament to the strength found in vulnerability and the miraculous potential for change that dwells within us all.

The Seeker's Quest for Change

The Seeker was once an ordinary individual, caught in the mundane rhythm of daily life. Each day blurred into the next—a cycle of work, obligations, and fleeting moments of joy that felt insufficient to fill an underlying void. Deep within, The Seeker felt an urge to break free, a flicker of hope that whispered of possibilities beyond the confines of routine. Yet, the prospect of change was daunting. Fear crept in, whispering doubts that stifled a voice longing to be heard.

One fateful day acted as a catalyst: The Seeker stumbled upon an old journal buried beneath a stack of forgotten books in the attic. Flipping through the pages, a wave of nostalgia washed over her. The wisps of dreams she had written in her younger years leaped off the page—ambitions of travel, passion for art, and the desire to connect with people deeply. "What happened to me?" she pondered, caught between reminiscing about a past full of aspiration and a present steeped in mediocrity.

That evening, as the sun began to set, enveloping the room in hues of lavender and gold, The Seeker Chose to sit in stillness. With each breath, she unearthed the courage to acknowledge her discontent. Gripped by vulnerability, she asked herself profound questions: What did she truly want? What did fulfillment look like? Each query led her deeper into a well of uncertainty but also unveiled a glimmer of hope—a chance to rekindle her passion for life.

Embracing this discomfort, she drafted her intentions. On a fresh page in the journal, a list emerged. She sought to create an art portfolio, travel to countries she had only dreamed of, and cultivate deeper relationships. This act marked the beginning of her transformative journey—a CHOICE that required vulnerability and a willingness to confront both her fears and aspirations head-on.

The Mentor's Insight on Embracing Change

In contrast, the narrative of The Mentor reveals wisdom amassed through years of experience. Once, The Mentor, too, had faced daunting CHOICES and transformations. Guided by a restless spirit, he had embarked on his own journey of self-discovery, cracking open the shell of his insecurities to emerge as the individual he had become.

A serene presence, The Mentor recalled a pivotal moment in his life where transformation was essential. After years of building a career that, from the outside, seemed perfect, he found himself teetering on the edge of discontent. Late nights at the office and weekends filled with networking left him feeling hollow. Despite the external accolades, he was not aligned with his true self; something profound was missing.

It was during a casual discussion with a mentee that a spark ignited. His mentee spoke of passion projects and taking bold steps into the unknown—the very essence of living authentically. As he listened, The Mentor felt a wave of vulnerability wash over him, keenly aware of the dissonance between the life he led and the life he truly yearned for. The CHOICE was this: remain within the confines of safety or take a leap into uncertainty.

With courage as his ally, The Mentor embraced that vulnerability, ultimately Choosing to pivot his career toward passions that aligned more closely with his values. He took small yet deliberate steps—starting a community workshop to share his knowledge and promote creativity, and mentoring those who seemed lost in their own transitions. In sharing his truth, he, too, transformed; his vulnerability resonated with others, creating connections that proved to be both healing and empowering.

The Interplay of Courage and Vulnerability

Both The Seeker and The Mentor illuminate the intricate dance between courage and vulnerability. It's within those moments of discomfort—where insecurities surface and the possibility of failure lurks—that true transformation unfolds. Vulnerability may feel like weakness to some, but it is, in essence, an invitation for authenticity and self-exploration. To embrace transformation, we must all confront the uncomfortable emotions that arise when we seek to change.

As The Seeker began sharing her intentions and aspirations, she realized she wasn't alone. Gathering with others who had also embarked on their journeys of self-discovery, she fostered a community infused with mutual support. They encouraged one another, shared triumphs and struggles, and collectively grew in courage to step outside familiar confines.

The Mentor mirrored this experience within his community workshops. Participants, once shy and reserved, began sharing their ideas, experiences, and vulnerabilities. The more they expressed their true selves, the greater the connection blossomed. They forged a network of empowerment, inspiring each other to take further leaps toward their aspirations.

Choosing to transform often necessitates a shift in perspective. Both characters demonstrated that the act of vulnerability didn't diminish their strength; rather, it increased their capacity to connect with others. They discovered that learning to embrace the idea of revealing their true selves— selves that carried imperfections—was, in fact, the cornerstone of genuine relationships, fostering an environment where transformation could thrive.

Restoring the Spirit through Self-Discovery

As weeks turned into months, The Seeker continued to evolve. Guided by the CHOICE to pursue her passions, she explored different art forms, experimented with styles, and began showcasing her work. Each piece crafted was not just art; it was a declaration of her journey, a canvas illustrating sections of her soul.

On an evening when vulnerability struck anew, she faced the fear of judgment. What if no one appreciated her work? What if they dismissed her as an amateur? Yet, she pressed through. The exhibition she organized felt as daunting as stepping into the ring of a boxing match. Outside, the world buzzed with expectations, but inside, she remained resolute.

With each passing conversation, as compliments flowed and people connected with her creations, she came face-to-face with the powerful transformation that occurs when you embrace your truth. The overwhelming validation from her community ignited a new flame within her. She was no longer merely a Seeker; she was a creator, a storyteller, embodying transformation through her art. Every brushstroke reflected a struggle, a redemption, intertwining her journey with others.

Simultaneously, The Mentor felt renewed as he observed the growth within his community. Through mentoring, he not only helped ignite change in others but also found that each story shared acted as a mirror, showcasing the ongoing transformation within himself. The act of pouring into others allowed him to tend to the roots of his own growth—acknowledging the importance of legacy and purpose in his life.

This reciprocal journey underscored the essential truth: the transformative power of change is inherently multifaceted and interconnected. Through vulnerability and courage, we do not merely change ourselves; we intertwine our paths with others, creating a richer tapestry woven from collective experiences and shared stories.

Celebrating the Journey of Transformation

With time, both The Seeker and The Mentor learned to celebrate not just the outcomes of their CHOICES, but the entire journey toward transformation. They embraced milestones as markers of progress—each step taken was a reason to celebrate. For The Seeker, every finished artwork represented a triumph, even the ones that didn't garner acclaim. For The Mentor, witnessing his mentees flourish marked moments of joy and hope.

Through micro-celebrations in their lives, they discovered that transformation is not solely about reaching a destination; it is about appreciating the beauty and lessons that arise throughout the winding journey. This revelation became a pivotal part of their practice—self-celebration, mindfulness, and gratitude allowed each to remain grounded amidst the storms of life and uncertainty that transformation often brings.

As the narratives interwove, they began to share reflections on their journeys during community gatherings. They scheduled moments to express gratitude and appreciation, entwining their growth with recognition of each other's contributions. In fostering collective recognition, both The Seeker and The Mentor found that each narrative belonged within a larger story, and together, they celebrated the creation of a collective anthem of change, courage, and transformation.

The Lasting Impact of Transformation

Ultimately, embracing transformation is not a solitary act; it echoes across time and space, extending far beyond the individual. It reveals the interconnectedness of communities, illustrating how changes in one person can resonate in ripple effects across many others. The Seeker's CHOICE sparked inspiration in her community, encouraging others to pursue their passions, mirrored in The Mentor's teachings that empowered individuals to craft their own narratives.

Together, they transformed landscapes of despair into realms of possibility, and as they journeyed along their respective paths, they inspired others to take leaps of courage in their own lives. They became change agents, capable of instilling hope and motivating transformation beyond their immediate circles.

Whether it is The Seeker or The Mentor, each story demonstrates a universal truth: the power we hold through our CHOICES transcends our own lives. The act of embracing transformation serves as a beacon of light for others residing in shadows of uncertainty. It reminds each of us that while the journey begins within, its influence stretches outward, creating a beautiful and lasting legacy anchored in courage, vulnerability, and unwavering hope for brighter days ahead.

In the quiet undertones of life, the echoes of CHOICE remain, dancing like leaves in the wind. Every decision shapes not only our own evolution but also the world around us. As we press forward together, let us commit to embracing the power of transformation that lies in the CHOICES we make. Let us inspire one another along the way, crafting rich tapestries of growth and courage that celebrate both the individual and the collective, leaving an indelible mark on generations to come.

Steps Toward Choosing Change

Choosing change is a powerful act, and it begins with the deliberate CHOICES we make in our daily lives. As we navigate the complexity of existence, implementing personal transformations can feel overwhelming. However, by breaking it down into actionable steps, we can create a clear pathway toward the change we desire. In this subchapter, we will explore practical methods for enacting change through deliberate CHOICES, providing you with reflective exercises and bullet-point lists of strategies to implement in your journey.

1. Identify Your Desire for Change

- **Reflect on Your Current State**

  Take a moment to pause and think about your life as it stands today. What aspects do you love? What would you like to change?

  o Write down three things that bring you joy.

  o Write down three aspects of your life that you feel are holding you back.

  o Reflect on how you feel about these areas. What emotions arise?

2. Define Clear Goals

- **Set Specific and Measurable Goals**

  Once you have identified what you want to change, it is essential to articulate this desire in specific terms.

  o Write a goal statement. For example, "I want to improve my physical health by exercising three times a week for 30 minutes."

- o Ensure your goals are measurable. Rather than saying, "I want to eat healthier," specify, "I will include two servings of vegetables in my meals each day."

3. Understand Your Motivations

- **Dig Deep into Your 'Why'**

Understanding what motivates you to change is critical. This provides the fuel needed to maintain momentum.

- o Write down your reasons for wanting to initiate this change.
- o Ask yourself questions:
  - Why is this change important to me?
  - How will my life be different once I make this change?

4. Break Down the Steps

- **Create an Action Plan**

Large, overarching goals can often feel intimidating. Breaking them down into manageable steps can ease this pressure.

- o Create a list of actionable steps required to achieve your goal. For instance, if your goal is to run a marathon, your steps might include:

    1. Research training schedules.

    2. Buy running shoes.

    3. Start with short runs.

- o **Reflect**: How can you divide each step further into daily tasks?

5. Establish a Timeline

- **Create Deadlines**

Setting a timeline can help you stay accountable and track progress.

- o Assign specific deadlines to your actionable steps. For instance, "I will complete week one of my training schedule by [date]."

- o Use a calendar or planner to jot down these deadlines.

6. Find Accountability

- **Engage a Support System**

Change is often easier when you involve others. Finding accountability can inspire and motivate you.

- o Share your goals with a friend or family member who can check in on your progress.
- o Consider joining a group or community related to your goal, such as a workout class or a book club.

7. Embrace Reflection

- **Cultivate a Habit of Self-Reflection**

Regularly assessing your progress can help you adjust your approach if necessary.

- o Keep a journal where you document your journey. Reflect on your successes and setbacks.
- o Set aside time weekly to review what has worked well and what may need revisiting.

8. Celebrate Progress

- **Acknowledge Small Victories**

Recognizing progress, no matter how small, helps maintain motivation.

o   Make a list of small milestones and reward
    yourself for achieving them.

o   Reflect on how these victories contribute to
    your larger goal.

9. Manage Setbacks

- **Prepare for Challenges**

Change is rarely linear; expect hurdles along the way.

o   Anticipate potential challenges you may face.
    How do you plan to overcome them?

o   Develop coping strategies in advance. This
    might involve taking a break or seeking
    additional help.

10. Maintain Flexibility

- **Adapt and Evolve**

As you journey toward change, allow yourself to adapt
your goals and approaches as needed.

o   Regularly assess whether your goals still align
    with your values and desires. Adjust as
    necessary.

o   Be open to new opportunities that may arise in

your path—they may lead you to unforeseen but desirable changes.

11. Visualize Your Future Self

- **Engage in Visualization Exercises**

Visualization is a powerful technique to reinforce your commitment to change.

  - Create a vision board with images or words that represent the life you want to create. Place it somewhere you can see it daily.

  - Spend time in meditation or quiet reflection, picturing yourself having achieved your goals. How does it feel?

12. Practice Mindfulness

- **Stay Present in Your Journey**

Mindfulness encourages you to be present, helping reduce anxiety related to change.

  - Incorporate mindfulness exercises into your routine, such as meditation or mindful breathing.

  - Reflect daily on your feelings as you move

through the process of change, accepting the range of emotions that arise.

13. Seek Resources

- **Use Books, Workshops, and Online Courses**

Educating yourself on your chosen area of change can provide invaluable insights.

   o Identify books or resources relevant to your goals—these could provide strategies, inspiration, and guidance.

   o Participate in workshops or online classes where you can learn from others who have embarked on similar journeys.

14. Commit to Continuous Learning

- **Adopt a Growth Mindset**

Each step of your transformation is an opportunity for learning and growth.

   o Embrace a mindset that treats setbacks as learning experiences. Ask yourself, "What can I learn from this?"

   o Celebrate your courage to embrace change and

keep an open heart for future challenges.

15. Reassess Regularly

- **Evaluate Your Progress**

  Make it a habit to look back and review your progress periodically.

  - Schedule monthly check-ins where you reflect on your journey. What has changed? How do you feel about it?

  - Identify areas you want to focus on moving forward, and adjust your action plan accordingly.

As you implement these strategies, remember that Choosing change is a journey, not a destination. Each step you take toward personal transformation is significant, paving the way for not only a new chapter in your life but also fostering deeper awareness of your CHOICES as a gift from God.

Change can be daunting, yet it is also an opportunity for growth. With every CHOICE, you are crafting the life you envision and deserve. Embrace the process, knowing that each step is part of a beautiful tapestry woven with intention and love.

Sustaining Change

In the journey of life, change is inevitable. We often possess the courage to initiate change, but the challenge lies in sustaining that change over time. Just like a seed buried deep within the soil, change requires nurturing, patience, and a particular set of conditions to thrive and grow. Sustaining change involves commitment—an unwavering resolve to hold onto the transformation we have achieved through our CHOICES while navigating the complexities of life.

To understand how to maintain change, we must first reflect on what it means to change. Change can manifest in myriad forms. It could be a change in habit, mindset, or lifestyle. Perhaps you have successfully quit smoking, adopted a healthier diet, or shifted to a more positive outlook on life. At the beginning of these journeys, motivation often flows abundantly. We are exhilarated by the prospect of transformation, fueled by visions of who we might become and what we might accomplish.

However, as the initial thrill begins to fade, the reality of sustaining these changes sets in. This might manifest in feelings of doubt, frustration, or even defeat. Many people oscillate between periods of motivation and procrastination, feeling stuck in a loop of desire but lacking the means to hold themselves accountable. It is here, in this uncomfortable space, that the importance of intentionality comes into play. To foster lasting change, we must engage in deliberate actions that align with our goals.

Self-assessment tools can be incredibly valuable in this process. They provide structured frameworks for reflection, facilitating a deeper understanding of our progress and revealing areas needing more attention. Consider introducing a regular practice of journaling about your thoughts and feelings regarding the change you are trying to sustain. Write about your successes, however small, and create space for your struggles without judgment. Seeking to understand your emotional landscape will empower you to recognize patterns and triggers that impact your ability to maintain changes.

For instance, if you've Chosen to exercise regularly, document how you feel before and after your workouts. Examine the motivation behind your CHOICE to begin this journey. Are you doing it for health reasons, or are you trying to fit a particular image? Are there days when your motivation wanes? What external factors affect your commitment? Engaging in such reflective practices will allow you to clarify your intentions, reinforcing your commitment to the path you've Chosen.

In addition to self-reflection, incorporating accountability methods can significantly enhance your capacity to sustain change. Accountability can take many forms—finding an accountability partner or a mentor, joining a support group, or even utilizing social media platforms to share your goals. There's a profound strength found in community and shared experiences. When you openly share your journey, you invite others in, creating a network of support that can uplift you during moments of doubt.

The power of communal accountability cannot be understated. Consider the story of Maya, a young woman who aspired to lose weight after years of struggling with body image issues. Initially, her motivation came from a profound desire for change; however, as time progressed, she began to falter. Rather than succumb to defeat, Maya Chose to join an online support group dedicated to healthy living. By connecting with others on similar journeys, she found a renewed sense of purpose. Each week, the group would set collective goals and celebrate individual achievements, helping her to stay on track and encourage her shared commitment.

Life undeniably presents obstacles that threaten our

stability. And while emotional resilience plays a part, cultivating a holistic strategy is essential. Building supportive routines into your life can safeguard against periods of vulnerability. Rituals surrounding your CHOICES help anchor you, allowing you to navigate the ebbs and flows of motivation with greater ease.

For example, if you are focusing on a more intentional lifestyle, establish routines that nurture this shift. You might designate time each morning for mindful meditation, exercise, or meal prep. By incorporating new habits into your daily life, you begin to rewire your brain to favor these changes. It requires conscious effort at first, much like learning to ride a bike. Initially, it may feel clumsy or unnatural, but with practice, it becomes second nature.

Additionally, habit stacking—a term popularized in habits literature—refers to the technique of linking new habits to existing ones. For instance, if you already have a habit of enjoying a morning coffee, you could add a reflection practice to that time. As the coffee brews, take a few moments to contemplate your progress toward your change. This method strengthens the anchoring of your new behavior, increasing the likelihood of sustained commitment. Consistency, as mentioned, is crucial.

Real-life examples abound of individuals who have achieved sustainable change through a combination of self-assessment, accountability, supportive environments, and daily rituals. Consider James, a former athlete who succumbed to injuries that forced him to retire from professional sports. Faced with the impending loss of a familiar identity, James Chose to coach youth sports in his community, a decision born out of passion for nurturing the next generation. This CHOICE was transformative, but sustaining that change required more than his initial enthusiasm.

James implemented regular self-check-ins, assessing his emotional attachment to his athletic identity while embracing his role as a mentor. He initiated weekly meetings with fellow coaches to share experiences, refining their techniques and uplifting one another. These sessions not only fortified their bonds but also ingrained accountability into his new role.

The journey of change is deeply personal, and sometimes it involves confronting uncomfortable truths. Sustaining change demands that we unearth the layers of our psyche, laying bare fears, insecurities, and doubts that can inhibit our progress. It is essential to approach this discovery with compassion, allowing yourself the grace to be imperfect. There will be days when you stumble, when your resolve falters, and that's okay. The beauty of sustaining change is in the process, not merely the endpoint.

When those moments arise, do not shy away from seeking support. As previously mentioned, having companions on this journey can be transformative. Your accountability partners or supportive friends can provide powerful encouragement, reminding you of the strength you possess and the commitment you made to yourself. And in those shared hardships, bonds often deepen, creating a rich tapestry of human connection and resilience.

Visualization exercises can also be beneficial tools for sustaining change. Envision your future self—the version of you who has succeeded in this journey. What will your life look like? How will you feel? What habits will you embody? By vividly painting this picture in your mind, you create a compelling vision that serves as a guiding beacon, illuminating the way even when the path becomes murky.

Engaging with your future self allows you to forge a deeper commitment to your CHOICES. Consider writing a letter to this envisioned version of yourself, articulating your goals, dreams, and aspirations. What advice do you think they would give you in times of struggle? How would they challenge you to keep moving forward? The more emotionally charged and clear this vision, the more aligned your actions will become with this ideal.

Throughout this journey, it is vital to celebrate progress, however incremental. Each step forward is a testament to your dedication and an affirmation of how far you've come. Acknowledge the milestones and victories that arise along the way—whether it's hitting the gym consistently for a month or making strides in a personal project. These celebrations foster motivation, propelling you through the tougher times.

In conclusion, sustaining change ultimately hinges on a commitment to nurturing your holistic approach to transformation. By employing self-assessment tools, seeking accountability, establishing supportive routines, and forging a vivid connection with your future aspirations, you create a solid foundation upon which lasting change can flourish. Remember, it is a journey, not a destination. Your CHOICES shape your path, and it's the consistent effort that will lead you to the transformation you seek. Embrace the process, and trust in your capacity to navigate the tides of change with resilience.

As you embark on this journey, know that you are not

alone. There exists a community of fellow travelers, each with their own tales of ups and downs, and together, you can sustain the vibrant changes that have the power to transform not just your life, but ripples that will extend far beyond you into the world.

Collective CHOICES

Interconnected Lives

In the grand tapestry of life, each individual thread contributes to a larger design, a pattern that intertwines with countless others. Every CHOICE made is a pivotal brushstroke in the artwork of existence, creating ripples that extend far beyond our immediate surroundings. As we journey through our lives, it's essential to recognize the profound impact our CHOICES make not only on our own existence but also on the lives of those around us. This subchapter will explore the concept of interconnectedness, illustrating how our CHOICES can foster harmony, growth, and transformation within our communities and the world at large.

Let us begin with a simple yet powerful tale of a small town named Willow Creek, where each resident's action intricately shaped the community's essence. Situated in a lush valley, Willow Creek thrived on the agricultural richness of its land, but what truly nourished it were the relationships among its people. Here, neighbors were more than just people living next door; they were integral cogs in a collective machine, each piece serving a unique role that contributed to the town's vitality.

In this town lived a woman named Clara, a vibrant local artist whose murals brought color to otherwise dreary buildings. One day, Clara Chose to paint a mural depicting an interconnected universe, featuring trees that intertwined their roots, flowers that danced together in the wind, and animals that scurried beneath a vast sky filled with stars. Inspired by her vision, Clara invited her fellow townsfolk to contribute. She envisioned this mural as a collaborative project that would visually encapsulate the beauty of their interconnected lives.

As the townsfolk gathered to paint, friendships blossomed,

and bonds were strengthened. Clara noticed how the elderly shared stories of their youth with the children, speaking of the importance of kindness, patience, and respect within the community. It was a moment where individuals came together, transcending their differences, all contributing to a collective vision that would last for generations. The children, excited as they mixed bright pigments, learned the value of teamwork, and in those colors, they painted their futures filled with dreams.

The mural became a symbol of their unity, serving as a reminder of how individual parts could create a stunning whole. This is the beauty of collective CHOICE: when people Choose to come together, magic happens. The intrinsic connections made during the mural project rippled through the community, resulting in increased collaboration among local businesses, a revival of neighborhood events, and a renewed sense of belonging. Clara had unveiled a truth that everyone felt but never articulated: their CHOICES mattered, and collectively, they created a significant impact.

The interconnectedness experienced in Willow Creek reminds us that every CHOICE is a thread weaving through a larger fabric, affecting the lives of others in ways we may not immediately perceive. A CHOICE as seemingly small as

219

helping a neighbor can spark a chain reaction of kindness that encapsulates an entire community. For every action, there is a reaction, and as members of our social fabric, we must acknowledge how our CHOICES send waves through the interconnected lives of others.

Beyond the microcosm of Willow Creek lies a broader world where our collective CHOICES wield immense influence. Consider the global impact of individual CHOICES related to consumerism, environmental sustainability, or social justice. In our world, every purchase we make reverberates through a network of farmers, manufacturers, transporters, and retailers. A CHOICE to buy locally produced goods can uplift communities, bolster local economies, and foster a sustainable relationship with the environment. Conversely, a CHOICE to purchase from distant corporations can contribute to economic disparities and environmental degradation.

Let's take the story of Samuel, a young man from a bustling city who made a conscious CHOICE to change his consumption habits. Disillusioned by the omnipresence of major corporations, he Chose to support local artisans and sustainable businesses. Samuel's journey began when he stumbled upon a farmer's market nestled at the heart of his neighborhood. Intrigued by the vibrant displays of homegrown fruits and vegetables, he struck up conversations with local farmers. These interactions made him realize that his CHOICES could influence not just his own life but also the livelihoods of those individuals who poured their hearts into producing quality, sustainable food.

By Choosing to buy from local markets, Samuel became part of a movement that revived agricultural traditions, promoted ethical practices, and encouraged a robust local economy. The farmers, in turn, could invest in sustainable farming methods, ensuring the land remained fertile for future generations. Samuel's ripple effect didn't stop there; he encouraged his friends to join him, leading to a small community of conscious consumers, each CHOICE feeding the growth of this sustainable ecosystem.

This narrative illustrates the lesson that individual CHOICES, when collected together, form powerful movements, altering landscapes and reshaping communities. Just as Clara's mural in Willow Creek united her neighbors, Samuel's CHOICES inspired a cohort of individuals to reflect on their purchasing decisions and their broader consequences. Together, their voices became a collective affirmation that consumer CHOICES can shape an interconnected world.

The complexities of interconnected lives extend into every sphere of our existence. In the realm of social justice, the impact of personal CHOICES can also be monumental. Stories from individuals fighting for equality highlight how collective action derived from individual CHOICES mobilizes change. Consider Emma, a university student whose passion for equality led her to become involved in activism against systemic racism. She began her journey by Choosing to educate herself about issues affecting marginalized communities and discussing these topics with peers.

Emma organized workshops focused on anti-racism, encouraging her classmates to share their perspectives and experiences. Her CHOICE to engage became a catalyst, sparking deeper conversations that transcended the classroom. This awareness spread across campus, leading to larger student movements advocating for institutional reforms, inclusivity, and representation.

In this instance, Emma's CHOICE to act not only impacted her immediate community but also transcended it, inspiring alumni to join the cause and prompting administrative changes at the university level. This narrative illustrates the profound connection between individual CHOICE and systemic change—a reminder that when one person Chooses to take a stand, ripples of consequence can influence entire institutions and societies.

To illustrate the interconnectedness theme further, let us visit the world of environmental advocacy. The global climate crisis provides a striking example of how our collective CHOICES matter. Every CHOICE made—whether to recycle, conserve resources, or support clean energy projects—shapes the world we inhabit. These small actions may seem insignificant on their own, but collectively they can alter the trajectory of climate change.

An impactful narrative is that of an ecological group known as Earth Guardians. Founded by a community of young activists, they Chose to engage in climate action by advocating for environmental education in schools. Their mission was clear: inspire the next generation to understand the significance of caring for the planet. By Championing these initiatives, they emphasized that each child's CHOICES regarding resource use or conservation would ripple out, building sustainability into community culture.

As Earth Guardians expanded their reach, they faced challenges but also discovered how interconnected their pursuit for change was to other causes. Their advocacy aligned with social equity movements, revealing that environmental degradation often disproportionately affects marginalized communities. Understanding this connection broadened their mission, creating an intersectional approach that embraced diverse perspectives.

By participating in this grassroots movement, the young activists learned firsthand how interconnected lives are woven together through common goals and shared responsibilities. Through collective CHOICE, they became part of a larger coalition advocating for policy changes at local and national levels, showcasing the expansive reach of their decisions.

In reflecting on interconnected lives, one cannot ignore the digital age's influence on our personal CHOICES and their global consequences. Social media platforms allow individuals to voice opinions, share experiences, and mobilize movements with unprecedented ease. The story of the Arab Spring illustrates how the CHOICES made by individuals to speak out against oppressive regimes led to massive uprisings and significant political reform across the Middle East.

Through social media, people documented their struggles, shared their stories, and organized protests, creating an instantaneous wave of solidarity that overcame geographical boundaries. These individuals, Choosing to stand up for their rights, ignited collective action that no longer remained confined to individual communities; they demonstrated how the CHOICES made in one part of the world can inspire movements globally. Each livestreamed event, hashtag, and shared post added fuel to a fire of collective resistance, showcasing the beauty of interconnected lives powered by shared struggles and aspirations.

Yet, it is crucial to recognize that not all ripples create waves of positive change. Some CHOICES can lead to division and discord, especially in a world fueled by misinformation and fear. Reflecting on the dynamics of social media, it becomes apparent how the same platforms that connect us can also amplify division and hostility. In such instances, individual CHOICES to propagate misinformation or engage in polarizing rhetoric can produce harmful repercussions that sever the threads connecting us.

For example, consider the rise of misinformation on health topics during crises like pandemics. Personal CHOICES to share misleading information can lead to confusion, mistrust, and detrimental health decisions. When individuals Choose to spread unverified claims, they contribute to waves of fear that ripple through their communities, negatively impacting public health responses and individual well-being.

Thus, we must take a moment to reflect on our own decision-making processes. How consciously are we Choosing to engage in our communities, whether through activism, consumer preferences, or social interactions? The responsibility of CHOICE lies within us, compelling us to navigate our actions with awareness of their potential impact.

While the beauty of interconnected lives pulses through stories of unity, growth, and collective innovation, it also serves as a cautionary tale about the darker consequences of our CHOICES. Every person has the power to contribute to a narrative of healing or harm. The interconnectedness of lives offers a vast canvas upon which to paint future realities, urging us toward intentional, conscious CHOICES that can sow the seeds of positive impact rather than division.

In closing, let us reflect on the multifaceted nature of our CHOICES and the ways they reverberate through the lives of others. Each CHOICE, no matter how small or seemingly insignificant, becomes a thread in our collective story. We each hold the brush, capable of coloring the world with vibrant CHOICES that enrich, connect, and uplift one another.

To embody this interconnectedness, we must Choose empathy, creativity, and intention. Like Clara's mural, we have the power to showcase the beauty of community woven from disparate threads of existence. Whether through supporting local businesses, standing up for social justice, advocating for environmental sustainability, or fostering meaningful dialogue, our CHOICES can transform lives, build bridges, and inspire generations. Together, as we weave our stories into the great tapestry of life, let us Choose to act with love, compassion, and a deep understanding of the interconnectedness we share.

Building Shared Narratives

In the woven fabric of our lives, we find that individual CHOICES are but threads in a grand tapestry, but when we look closely, it becomes evident that the strongest and most vibrant patterns arise from collective CHOICES. As individuals, we are often quick to think that our CHOICES are solitary acts, yet the reality is that we are seldom alone in our decision-making. Every CHOICE we make has the potential to ripple outward, affecting not just ourselves, but our families, communities, and even the world at large.

Within families, a shared narrative often emerges from the

CHOICES made around the dinner table. Consider, for instance, a family that Chooses to spend time volunteering at a local shelter. This CHOICE does not merely impact those who receive the service; it shapes the family's identity, instilling values of service, kindness, and empathy in its members. Over time, these shared experiences knit them closer together, creating a narrative of compassion that transcends the immediate act of giving. Each family story— each collective CHOICE—builds on the last, evolving and enhancing their legacy.

Communities, too, thrive on shared narratives that are woven from collective CHOICES made in the face of common challenges. Examples abound, from neighborhood clean-up days to community gardens, where residents band together to revitalize their surroundings. These coordinated efforts serve as landmarks of what is possible when individuals come together, showcasing the power of unity and collaboration.

Consider a small town where a group of citizens becomes concerned about the lack of green spaces for families to enjoy. Rather than succumbing to apathy or individual despair, they convene, brainstorming solutions and collaborating with local authorities. Their collective CHOICE to advocate for a community park leads to action that not only beautifies their neighborhood but also fosters connections among residents. Soon, children laugh as they play, parents bond over shared picnics, and an intergenerational sense of belonging flourishes. As stories of friendships formed and memories created in the park spread, a shared narrative of resilience and collaboration emerges, one that inspires future generations.

When we examine larger societal movements, the impact of collective CHOICES is even more pronounced. The civil rights movement provides a poignant example: Individuals from diverse backgrounds made the powerful CHOICE to stand together against oppression, dreaming of a more equitable society. Their shared narrative transformed into a legacy of courage, with each CHOICE to march, to speak out, and to act collectively contributing to monumental change. The echoes of their CHOICES continue to resonate today, showcasing the profound influence of building shared narratives.

As we consider these examples, it is essential to recognize that we, too, have the capacity to engage in similar collective CHOICES. Building shared narratives starts with identifying the groups we belong to, be they families, friendship circles, workplace teams, or community organizations. Reflecting on these connections encourages us to assess how our collective CHOICES shape our identities and values.

To assist in this exploration, take the following exercise:

1. Make a list of the groups to which you belong. This could include family, friends, colleagues, community organizations, or even online groups that share common interests.

2. For each group, jot down a few significant CHOICES that you remember being made collectively. What were the CHOICES? What led to these decisions? How did the outcome shape the group's identity or values?

3. Reflect on how these narratives have impacted you personally. How have they influenced your beliefs, behaviors, or even your own CHOICES?

This exercise is not merely a reflective activity; it is a vital step in uncovering the thematic threads that connect us to others. As you begin to map out the shared narratives within your life, consider how they contribute to a greater communal identity. The CHOICES made within our groups—whether in celebration, mourning, or activism—define not only our immediate circles but echo into wider societal realms.

Often, shared narratives are birthed out of necessity.

During times of crisis, people tend to come together, forming alliances that may not have previously existed. A poignant example is during natural disasters, where communities rally to support one another, Choosing to bring food and supplies to those affected or participating in recovery efforts. These collective CHOICES illustrate not only the resilience of the human spirit but also the innate desire to belong and care for one another.

The COVID-19 pandemic acted as a global crucible of collective decision-making. Different communities approached the crisis in diverse ways, guided by shared narratives that shaped their resilience. Some Chose to prioritize public health measures, resulting in a collective narrative centered around safety and solidarity. Others made CHOICES driven by the desire to preserve their livelihoods, leading to narratives of defiance and dissent. In each case, the CHOICES made were influenced by a myriad of factors—cultural beliefs, economic realities, and social understanding.

As these narratives unfolded, they revealed deeper truths about human nature. We crave connection, understanding, and a sense of belonging, all of which can be found when we Choose together. The efforts undertaken by individuals within the same community can catalyze significant changes, often leading to more meaningfully crafted futures.

To explore this further, consider engaging with your groups in a shared decision-making process. Pick a topic of interest—perhaps how your workplace can contribute to sustainability initiatives or how your family might celebrate each other's milestones more intentionally. Gather input from everyone, and collaboratively Choose a course of action. Document the decision-making process and the final outcome, and reflect on how this shared narrative will influence your interactions moving forward.

As we cultivate shared narratives within these smaller groups, it is essential to broaden our understanding of collective identity. We live in a world filled with countless voices, cultures, and perspectives that all contribute to the larger human narrative. Within this context, collective CHOICES can unite us in the face of shared challenges.

The environmental movement exemplifies how collective narratives can transcend borders. Across the globe, individuals have Chosen to join forces to demand action against climate change—drawing on the shared narrative of stewardship and responsibility toward our planet. These collective CHOICES echo through marches, petitions, and local activism; they reinforce the notion that individual actions can contribute to a larger cause, encouraging others to join in and embrace their power.

Through this lens, we see how shared narratives shape not only our identities but also societal paradigms at large. As we reflect on our own communal engagements, we gain insight into the ways that collective CHOICES steer society toward progress. The ensuing momentum forms a tapestry of empathy, collaboration, and action that resonates beyond generations.

To embed this understanding further, consider another reflective exercise:

1. Choose a collective CHOICE that has influenced your life significantly, either positively or negatively. This could be a decision by a group you're part of or a broader movement that you followed.

2. Identify the values and beliefs that underpinned that CHOICE. What sense of purpose or collective identity did it foster?

3. Explore how this CHOICE has prompted personal growth or reflection in your life. How has it shaped your values, or how you see yourself within your

community?

As you immerse yourself in the intricacies of these narratives, you cultivate an invaluable skill: the ability to view CHOICES through the lens of collective impact. Recognizing that we are all interconnected emphasizes the power of empathy. Understanding how our CHOICES influence others fosters a deeper commitment to making decisions that benefit not just ourselves, but our families, communities, and society.

These narratives continue to evolve, illustrating how CHOICES can birth new identities and possibilities. Just as a story does not end with one event, neither does our ongoing tale of collective existence. As you engage in shared reflections, embrace the belief that each CHOICE contributes to a legacy—a legacy built on shared experiences, hard-earned lessons, and the potential for transformation.

The responsibility of documenting these narratives falls upon us as we continually navigate the web of influence we share with others. Consider writing down the significant collective CHOICES you've been part of. Capture the dialogues, the disappointments, the joys, and finally, the triumphs that emerge from these experiences. By doing so, we honor the myriad voices that have intertwined with our own, shaping the course of our lives.

Your narratives, along with others', can inspire future generations who will stand on the shoulders of our collective CHOICES. They may look back on these documented histories to understand what it means to stand together, to unite for a common cause, and to champion the love and kindness that fuels humanity's progress. In every family story, community effort, or global movement, there is a tapestry of shared CHOICES unfolding—a beautiful spectrum of human experience that nurtures hope for an interconnected future.

Ultimately, weaving these narratives serves not just to record who we are but to affirm who we wish to become. When we recognize the power of collective CHOICES, we embrace the courage to stand up for what we believe in. The CHOICES we make together can reshape not only our immediate surroundings but also the world at large. As we build shared narratives, we not only tell our stories; we become agents of change, building a legacy anchored in resilience, love, and profound connections.

In a world that often seeks to divide, our shared stories become a welcoming bridge, encouraging unity, understanding, and collaborative action. As stewards of these narratives, we have the tremendous opportunity to craft an extraordinary future, one CHOICE at a time.

Empathetic CHOICES

In the course of our lives, each CHOICE we make reverberates far beyond our immediate surroundings, influencing the lives of others in profound ways. As we navigate the intricacies of familial ties, friendships, and broader community interactions, it becomes increasingly clear that our CHOICES are woven into a larger tapestry of human experience. This interconnectedness underscores the moral responsibility we bear: our CHOICES have the power to uplift or to diminish, to connect or to isolate.

Empathy, defined as the ability to understand and share the feelings of another, serves as a vital guide in the decision-making process. It encourages us to step out of our individual perspectives and consider the impact of our CHOICES on those around us. When we practice empathy, we can make CHOICES that not only reflect our values but also resonate with others, fostering a sense of community and shared purpose.

Embracing Empathy in Decision-Making

To cultivate a culture of empathetic CHOICES, we must first understand the nuanced nature of empathy itself. Empathy goes beyond mere sympathy; it requires an active engagement with the emotions and experiences of others. This can manifest in various forms, including cognitive empathy, where we seek to understand another person's thoughts and perspectives, and emotional empathy, which involves sharing in their feelings as if they were our own.

To incorporate empathy into our decision-making, we can begin with three essential steps: awareness, reflection, and action.

Awareness: Recognizing Interconnectedness

The first step toward empathetic decision-making is to develop an awareness of our interconnectedness with others. This requires an understanding that we are part of a larger community and that our CHOICES impact not only ourselves but also those around us.

Begin by observing the interactions within your immediate environment. Notice how the CHOICES made by those around you influence your mood, your opportunities, and your relationships. Consider how your own CHOICES contribute to the dynamics within your community, whether at home, school, work, or any other social setting. This awareness can act as a catalyst for thinking more deeply about the implications of your CHOICES.

One practical exercise to enhance awareness involves keeping a daily journal of your CHOICES and their effects. Throughout a week, take note of CHOICES—both big and small—and reflect on how each one impacted those around you. For example, did a CHOICE to help a colleague with a project foster collaboration, or did a hurried response in a moment of stress create tension? By scrutinizing these moments, you begin to recognize the web of influence your CHOICES weave.

Reflection: Walking in Others' Shoes

Once you have cultivated an awareness of interconnectedness, the next step is reflection. This phase involves taking the time to consider how your CHOICES might affect others' lives. One powerful method to facilitate this reflection is to literally and figuratively "walk in another person's shoes."

Imagine the daily lives of those who populate your community: the single parent balancing work and caregiving, the elderly neighbor who longs for companionship, or the colleague who struggles with mental health challenges. How might your CHOICES alter their experiences? Will your CHOICE to volunteer, speak up during meetings, or simply offer a kind word contribute positively to their lives?

Engage in conversations with those around you to gain insight into their perspectives. Ask open-ended questions and listen actively. How do they feel respected or disrespected in their daily circumstances? What kind of support do they seek? This will help you build a deeper understanding of their needs and desires. This deeper connection is the foundation upon which empathetic decision-making is built.

Creating a Reflection Circle

To further enhance reflective practices, consider forming a "Reflection Circle" with friends, family, or coworkers. In these circles, members can share their personal experiences related to decision-making and the impacts of those CHOICES on their lives and communities. This group dialogue will not only foster empathy but also strengthen relationships through shared vulnerabilities. Collectively explore case studies or real-life scenarios where CHOICES had both positive and negative outcomes, analyzing the reasons behind each decision and its broader ramifications.

Action: Making CHOICES with Intention

The culmination of awareness and reflection leads to a powerful call to action. Empathetic CHOICES are not passive; they require conscious intention. This involves seeking to support and uplift others through your CHOICES, reinforcing the theme of accountability.

How can you convert empathy into action? Here are some practical steps to incorporate into your decision-making process:

1. **Seek Inclusive Perspectives:** When faced with CHOICES that affect others, actively seek out the voices of those who will be impacted. In workplaces, this may mean consulting a diverse group rather than relying on a select few. In community settings, invite feedback from marginalized voices who may be overlooked.

2. **Prioritize Compassionate CHOICES:** Allow compassion to guide your CHOICES. For example, consider how a CHOICE regarding resource allocation in a community project might impact

different groups. Choose options that would benefit the most vulnerable, even if it means sacrificing convenience for yourself.

3. **Practice Transparency and Communication:** Foster an environment where open communication about CHOICES is encouraged. Sharing the reasoning behind your CHOICES creates trust and invites collaboration. When others understand where you're coming from, they are more likely to feel included and valued.

4. **Respond to Feedback:** Embrace an attitude of humility and readiness to learn from others. When you receive feedback about your CHOICES—positive or negative—view it as an opportunity for growth. Apologize when necessary, seek forgiveness, and adjust your approach based on the insights gained. This reinforces a community culture of accountability.

5. **Model Empathy in the Community:** Use your voice to advocate for those who may not be heard. Engage in community service, mentor others, or participate in initiatives that promote social justice. Choosing to act as a model of empathy will inspire those around you

to make similar CHOICES.

Empathy in Collective CHOICES

The impact of empathetic CHOICES extends far beyond the individual, weaving a fabric of connectedness that enriches communities. When we prioritize empathetic decision-making, we foster an atmosphere of inclusiveness and support—one where everyone feels valued and heard.

In collective environments, whether they be workplaces, neighborhoods, or social groups, empathetic CHOICES provide a pathway toward collaboration and shared success. Organizations that promote empathetic decision-making tend to see higher employee satisfaction, increased team cohesion, and improved overall morale. This is because when individuals feel understood, they are more likely to contribute their best selves to the collective effort.

The Ripple Effect of Empathetic CHOICES

Empathetic CHOICES create ripples in the fabric of society, where one small act can lead to widespread change. Consider, for example, the greater impact of individuals Choosing to donate time to a local shelter. Each hour spent helping those in need not only makes a difference in the lives of the recipients but also fosters a culture of compassion among volunteers. This collective CHOICE cultivates a community where empathy and generosity are rewarded, leading to more individuals stepping forward.

The beauty of this ripple effect is that it extends infinitely; one empathetic CHOICE leads to another, inspiring a chain reaction of kindness. As people experience the richness of support and understanding, they are imbued with the desire to reciprocate, creating a cyclical pattern of positive CHOICES.

When empathy is embedded within a community, everyone benefits. We witness a nurturing environment where individuals feel emotionally safe and willing to take risks in their relationships and pursuits. This not only fortifies the social fabric but also enables resilience in the face of adversities.

Challenges in Empathetic Decision-Making

While the benefits of empathetic CHOICES are profound, engaging in this practice is not devoid of challenges. We live in a fast-paced world often inundated with self-interest and the pursuit of individualistic goals. The pressures to prioritize one's own needs can easily overshadow the connective nature of empathy.

Furthermore, societal biases can cloud our perceptions, leading to CHOICES that reinforce existing inequities. This is particularly evident in professional or community arenas where preconceived notions may influence how we view others and the CHOICES we make on their behalf. Being aware of these biases is crucial in amplifying empathy and ensuring that our CHOICES contribute to a more just society.

Overcoming Resistance to Empathy

When faced with resistance to empathetic CHOICES, it is vital to remember the potency of dialogue. Engaging in thoughtful conversations with those who disagree or have different life experiences can present opportunities for growth. Instead of retreating into polarization, open the floor for discussions that unpack different perspectives and validate feelings.

Furthermore, recognizing that empathy is a skill that can be cultivated over time can encourage individuals to practice in small, intentional ways. Start by focusing on one empathetic CHOICE each day. This could mean showing kindness to a stranger, listening deeply to a friend, or volunteering for a cause you care about. By building up these experiences, we develop the muscle of empathy, transforming it into a habitual part of our decision-making.

Creating Empathetic Communities

To solidify the legacy of empathetic CHOICES, we must actively work to build empathetic communities. This involves several key elements:

1. **Education and Training:** Implement programs that emphasize the importance of empathy, social responsibility, and community engagement. Schools and organizations can run workshops that explore how to make CHOICES that support others, reinforcing a foundational understanding early on.

2. **Encouraging Participation:** Offer platforms for community members to express their needs, concerns, and aspirations. This can include town hall meetings, focus groups, or feedback initiatives where individuals feel empowered to share their perspectives. The more involved people are in the decision-making process, the more ownership they will feel.

3. **Celebrating Empathetic Acts:** Highlight and celebrate individuals and groups who make empathetic CHOICES within the community. Recognizing these

efforts fosters a culture that values and promotes compassion, encouraging others to take similar steps.

4. **Mindfulness Practices:** Integrate mindfulness practices into community activities, creating space for reflection and connection. Mindfulness cultivates present-moment awareness and can enhance one's capacity for empathy. Consider organizing community meditation sessions or workshops that focus on empathy training.

Conclusion: A Call to Empathetic Action

The journey toward empathetic decision-making is a profound one, filled with learning, self-discovery, and meaningful connections. By understanding the implications of our CHOICES, embracing the interconnectedness of our communities, and committing to act with intention, we can forge a path toward a more compassionate world.

The call for empathetic CHOICES extends to each and every one of us. In a landscape marked by division and strife, let us strive to be beacons of empathy and kindness. Every small CHOICE we make can ripple outward, creating threads of connection and understanding. Together, as we cultivate empathy in our CHOICES, we can nurture the bonds that tie us to one another, enriching our collective experience and making our communities stronger and more resilient.

May we view each CHOICE as an opportunity to Choose understanding and compassion. As we embark on this journey of empathetic CHOICES, we are not merely shaping our individual experiences, but paving the way for a future grounded in dignity, respect, and love for one another.

Blessings of Being Intentional

Living with Purpose

In a world that often rushes by at an alarming pace, filled with obligations and distractions, the pursuit of a meaningful life can feel elusive. Amid the clamor of daily routines and societal expectations, intentionality emerges as a beacon—a guiding principle that helps individuals navigate life with purpose and clarity. Living with purpose not only enriches individual lives but also radiates outward, affecting families, communities, and the world at large. This journey begins with self-exploration, delving deep into personal values and desires.

At its core, intentionality calls for conscious decision-making; it urges us to become architects of our own lives rather than mere inhabitants. The simplicity of this message belies its profound implications. Each choice we make, whether trivial or monumental, shapes the narrative of our existence. To live intentionally is to be aware and deliberate in our decisions—an empowering practice that transforms the mundane into something meaningful.

The journey toward living with purpose often begins with self-reflection. Engaging in contemplative practices allows individuals to sift through the noise of daily life and discover their core values. These foundational principles serve as a compass, guiding decisions and actions in alignment with one's true self. Understanding what genuinely matters is crucial. Consider setting aside regular time for introspection, perhaps through journaling, meditation, or quiet contemplation. Such practices create sacred spaces where thoughts can flow freely, illuminating paths toward clarity.

As we delve deeper into our values, we must differentiate between what we genuinely desire and what external influences dictate. In a society rife with pressures—from social media portrayals of success to familial expectations—it's easy to lose sight of personal values. We may find ourselves chasing dreams that belong to others or conforming to societal norms at the expense of our happiness. A pivotal exercise to counter this disconnect is the "values assessment." Take a moment to list the values that resonate most deeply with you—love, freedom, creativity, responsibility, respect, or gratitude, to name a few. Upon reflection, consider how these values manifest in your daily life and decision-making processes.

As we continue our exploration, it's essential to ask: How do our choices align with these values? This inquiry lays the groundwork for intentional decision-making. Every day, we face myriad choices, each carrying weight and potential impact. Whether it's a decision about a job, relationships, or lifestyle habits, the nuance lies in the motivation behind these choices. To enhance intentionality, practice asking yourself the following questions:

1. Does this choice align with my core values?

2. Am I making this decision out of genuine desire or external pressure?

3. What is the potential impact of this choice on my life?

Armed with this reflective mindset, one begins to notice a remarkable shift in the quality of decisions. Each conscious choice creates a snowball effect, paving the way for greater fulfillment. When individuals decide from a place of authenticity, their actions resonate with their true selves, enabling them to embrace life's uncertainties with confidence.

With practice, living intentionally cultivates an environment ripe for growth and self-discovery. One practical approach is adopting habits that nurture this mindset. Start with small, intentional actions, such as prioritizing time for activities that align with your values. If creativity is fundamental to your spirit, allocate time to paint, write, or explore artistic avenues that ignite your passion. If nurturing relationships holds significance, reach out to loved ones and invest in meaningful conversations. Be deliberate in these actions, allowing them to flourish, as every intentional choice plants the seeds of a fulfilling life.

As readers embark on this transformative journey, they will likely encounter obstacles—moments of doubt, fear, and distraction. Embracing these challenges is an integral part of the process. Intentional living is not a linear path but a winding road, marked by both successes and setbacks. Recognizing fear as a natural companion rather than an enemy can empower individuals to confront their worries head-on. It's crucial to cultivate a relationship with fear where it becomes a motivator rather than a deterrent. Recognizing when fear stems from societal expectations or self-doubt can help individuals reclaim their authenticity.

In the face of obstacles, it is essential to revisit your core values. Grounding yourself in these values can serve as an anchor during turbulent times. Reflect on past experiences where lived values guided you through difficulty. Recounting these moments reaffirms the importance of deliberate choices and fortifies the belief that authentic living fosters resilience and growth.

As we increasingly prioritize intentional decision-making, the question arises: What impact can this have on our relationships with others? Living with purpose ripples outward, fostering deeper connections not only with oneself but also with the wider community. When individuals align their choices with authentic values, their genuine energy radiates, inspiring those around them to embark on similar journeys of intentionality. This shared exploration reinforces a culture of purpose, where collective efforts amplify individual intentions.

Consider the influence of daily interactions. Approach conversations and relationships with intention, actively choosing to engage with love, respect, and empathy. Aim to listen deeply and respond thoughtfully, which can dramatically enhance the quality of relationships. By being intentional in how we communicate and connect, we cultivate a supportive network that thrives on authenticity and understanding. This intentional approach can also transform environments, whether workplaces, communities, or families. Encourage shared values and collective goals that uplift the group, fostering a sense of belonging and commitment.

Furthermore, the practice of intentional living encompasses ethical considerations. Each choice we make can have broader implications, especially regarding social and environmental responsibilities. By incorporating this dimension into conscious decision-making, individuals can contribute positively to society and the world at large. From choosing sustainable products to participating in community initiatives, intentional choices build bridges between personal fulfillment and collective welfare.

As part of the journey toward living with purpose, it is paramount to think about long-term goals. Where do you envision yourself in five, ten, or twenty years? Write down these aspirations and align current choices with these future visions. Envision the journey as a series of stepping stones leading to desired outcomes. Recognize that goals can evolve, and being open to reinterpretation is vital in maintaining authenticity.

Guided visualization can be a helpful exercise in this aspect. Close your eyes and picture a life rooted in intention. What does it look like? What choices led you to this moment? How do you feel in this imagined reality? Allowing yourself to visualize a fulfilling future can stoke motivation and passion, propelling you toward your goals.

Additionally, accountability plays a crucial role in sustaining a purposeful life. Share your goals and intentions with trusted friends or mentors who encourage commitment and reflection. Regularly check in with one another to discuss progress, celebrate achievements, and reassess any misalignments. This collaborative approach nurtures a culture of growth and promotes collective responsibility for personal intentions.

Celebrating victories, regardless of size, is essential in reinforcing intentional living. Create rituals to acknowledge achievements—perhaps a monthly review session where you celebrate what went well and reevaluate what could be improved. This habitual reflection solidifies the practice of living with purpose, continuously intertwining aspirations with lived values.

As the chapter continues, the interplay between living with purpose and overall well-being warrants exploration. A commitment to intentional decision-making fosters resilience against life's inevitable challenges, often leading to enhanced mental, emotional, and physical health. The energy cultivated through living authentically radiates positivity, contributing to a more balanced and fulfilling life. When individuals engage with life from a place of intention, they are more likely to experience heightened satisfaction and joy.

Moreover, integrating gratitude into intentional living amplifies its enriching effects. Practicing gratitude allows individuals to acknowledge the beauty of everyday moments and choices, cultivating a sense of appreciation for life itself. Consider starting or ending each day with a gratitude journaling ritual, noting specific choices made that aligned with your values. This simple yet profound exercise helps individuals recognize the power of intentionality in their lives.

Ultimately, the journey toward living with purpose is a

lifelong endeavor. It requires continual reflection, adaptation, and a commitment to authenticity. The evolving nature of life encourages individuals to reassess choices as circumstances change, ensuring that intentions remain aligned with personal truths. Each decision is a stepping stone on a much larger path, leading to growth and transformation.

As we conclude this exploration of living with purpose, it becomes clear that intentionality fosters not only personal fulfillment but also a deeper understanding of our interconnectedness. When individuals choose to engage with life mindfully and authentically, they contribute to a ripple effect that enhances the fabric of their communities and the world.

So let us embark on this journey together—embracing the gifts of awareness, reflection, and intentional decision-making. Let us choose to live not merely to exist, but to thrive, to grow, and to make a meaningful impact on ourselves and those around us. By consciously crafting our lives, we come to appreciate that every choice, no matter how small, holds the potential to transform the ordinary into the extraordinary.

The Symphony of Intention

Life, in its essence, unfolds like a grand symphony. Each

moment, each decision, each relationship adds notes to our unique composition. While we may not always recognize it, our choices resonate like music, creating rhythms and harmonies that contribute to the overall melody of our existence. In this subchapter, we explore the idea of life as a symphony of intention, emphasizing how purposeful choices orchestrate a fulfilling narrative.

Imagine stepping into a concert hall. The lights dim, and an orchestra begins to tune its instruments. Each musician has spent years mastering their craft, their individual choices leading to this moment of collective beauty. As the conductor raises the baton and the first notes emerge, a narrative begins—a tapestry of sound that tells a story of love, loss, triumph, and hope. Each instrument, from the violins to the brass, plays a part, much like the choices we make in life, contributing to the depth and richness of our experiences.

To frame our life decisions as a musical composition serves not only as a metaphor but also as a guide for how we can consciously create harmony in our lives. Much like an orchestra requires a conductor to lead and harmonize the various sections, we must take on the role of conductor in our own lives, making intentional choices that resonate with our values and aspirations.

Consider the tale of Ana, a seasoned pianist who spent her early life mastering the keys. Her journey illustrates the power of intention. Each practice session she engaged in, every piece she chose to learn, became part of her life's melody. Ana's decisions were not merely about playing music; they were about crafting her identity. She sought out pieces that resonated with her heart—compositions that conveyed her emotions and experiences.

As she navigated life, Ana found that the music she played reflected her inner world. The joyful sonatas echoed her moments of elation, while the melancholic adagios conveyed her struggles and losses. Ana's conscious choice to infuse intention into her musical studies not only shaped her as an artist but also enriched her experiences. The choices of repertoire, performance venues, and even the audiences she played for all contributed to the symphony of her life.

To articulate our intentional choices, we can identify key themes that reflect our values and desires. Much like composers select motifs that represent different emotions, we can discern which choices resonate most deeply with our true selves. Take a moment to reflect: What themes dominate your life's music? Is it adventure, creativity, connection, or perhaps resilience? By identifying these key themes, we can navigate our choices with clarity, ensuring that we craft a life that sings to our soul.

Another compelling narrative is that of Marcus, a community organizer who understood the power of collective harmony. He orchestrated events that brought neighboring communities together, encouraging individuals to share stories, skills, and support. Each event was a movement in the symphony of community building, echoing the notes of connection, empathy, and transformation. By making intentional choices in how he facilitated these gatherings, Marcus created a space where diverse melodies could harmonize, building a rich and nuanced narrative of shared experience.

Marcus's choice to cultivate intentional relationships with fellow organizers and volunteers was key to the resonance of his endeavors. This led to growth in opportunities for outreach, support, and engagement, embodying the essence of unity through purposeful choices.

As we explore our own narratives, consider engaging in activities to delve into the melodies of your life. Start by making a list of significant choices you have made. Perhaps you moved to a new city for a job opportunity, chose to pursue a creative passion, or decided to volunteer at a local nonprofit. Reflect on these moments and ask yourself:

- What were the intentions behind those choices?

- How did they shape your journey?

- What emotions do you associate with these decisions?

By recalling these key choices, you may uncover themes that define your life's melody. Look for common threads—are they centered around connection, adventure, or service? Once you identify these motifs, you can actively embrace them, allowing your future choices to resonate with clarity and purpose.

In addition, consider journaling exercises focused on your life's symphony. Start by composing a "Life Symphony" timeline. Sketch out the significant events or choices that have impacted your life, and for each, note the feelings, lessons, or insights gained. This practice not only reinforces the understanding of your choices but also cultivates an appreciation for the melody that is uniquely yours.

Consider the allegorical representation of your life's music as well. If your life were a composition, what would each section sound like? Write down descriptions of the different movements:

1. **The Opening Crescendo**: The beginnings, the dreams, and aspirations that shaped young adulthood.

2. **The Adagio of Reflection**: Moments of introspection, learning from past mistakes, and growth.

3. **The Allegro of Adventure**: Your adventures, travels, and the excitement of trying new things.

4. **The Final Harmony**: Where you see yourself heading in the future.

As you explore the diversity of your life's composition, acknowledge that every sound—be it harmonious or discordant—contributes to your overall symphony. The dissonances, or challenges, you've faced are as vital as the harmonious chords; they provide contrast and depth, culminating in a more complex and relatable narrative.

As life continues to unfold, let us intentionally cultivate the music we create through our choices. Just as a symphony evolves through rehearsals, feedback, and performances, our lives can be enriched through reflection, reevaluation, and intentional practice.

Through conscious decision-making, you elevate the quality of your life's music. Embrace the lessons learned from

261

both joyous crescendos and sorrowful finales. They all contribute to the beauty of the entire composition. Consider how your life's melody intertwines with those around you—how your intentions ripple through your family, friendships, and wider community.

Let's now delve into the act of musical improvisation, a practice that encourages adapting our choices in response to the circumstances and experiences we encounter. While there is beauty in composing a deliberate piece, life often requires us to improvise. Embrace spontaneity, allow yourself to pivot gracefully, and let the moments inspire new melodies.

Much like an improvisational jazz performance, our life's soundtrack can transform unpredictably, producing sounds that can surprise us in delight or discomfort. When we confront the unexpected, we must rely on our instincts and values to guide us, weaving our intentions into spontaneous creation. Revisit moments in your life where you felt compelled to change direction suddenly. What did that teach you? How did those improvisational choices contribute to your current symphony?

Finally, let us celebrate the power of collaboration in our symphonic lives. Just as musicians come together to produce a symphony greater than the sum of its parts, we can harness the strength of our relationships and communities. Seek out those whose melodies complement yours. Collaborate, share, and grow together. Recognizing that we are all composers in each other's lives fosters collaboration; it cultivates a richer experience for all involved.

In conclusion, the symphony of intention invites us to embrace our choices as an orchestration of melody, rhythm, and harmony. Acknowledge the depth of your unique composition, and allow the themes that resonate with your authentic self to guide your journey.

With every decision made with purpose, bend the notes of your experiences toward beauty, connection, and fulfillment. Conduct your life with intention, and let your symphony be one that inspires others to tune into their own melodic possibilities.

Cultivating Mindfulness

In the journey of life, where the path is paved with choices big and small, cultivating mindfulness becomes a cornerstone for making intentional decisions. The pace of modern living often leads us to rush through our days, skimming the surface of experiences without truly engaging with them. Developing a mindfulness practice is crucial; it grounds us in the present, opens our hearts and minds to our intentions, and enhances our ability to make conscious choices.

Mindfulness is more than a trend; it's an age-old practice grounded in awareness and presence. At its core, mindfulness involves paying attention to our thoughts, feelings, and bodily sensations in a non-judgmental way. By creating a space for contemplation, we shift from automatic reactions to thoughtful responses. This practice serves as a bridge between our present selves and the choices we make, illuminating the intention behind our actions.

To cultivate mindfulness, we will explore three primary techniques—meditation, journaling, and daily affirmations. Each method offers unique benefits and can be tailored to fit individual lifestyles, making it easier to weave these practices into daily routines. Let us delve into these techniques, understand their significance, and engage in practical exercises that encourage a mindful existence.

Meditation: The Art of Stillness

Meditation is often seen as a cornerstone of mindfulness. It offers a structured approach to quieting the mind, allowing us to explore our inner landscapes. The practice encourages awareness of our thoughts and feelings, enabling us to observe without attachment. To begin cultivating this skill, one does not need to sit cross-legged on a mountaintop or commit significant time. Even a few minutes a day can enhance clarity and focus.

Let's explore accessible methods to integrate meditation into daily life.

1. The Breath Awareness Technique

Find a comfortable, quiet place to sit or lie down. Close your eyes and focus on your breath. Notice the sensation of air entering your nostrils and filling your lungs. As you exhale, imagine tension leaving your body. Allow your breath to be your anchor. When thoughts arise—perhaps about the past or future—gently acknowledge them and return your focus to your breath. Start with five minutes, gradually increasing the duration as you feel comfortable.

2. Guided Meditation

For those who find it challenging to quiet their minds, guided meditation offers a bridge into the practice. Countless resources are available online, from apps to YouTube channels dedicated to this art. Choose a meditation that resonates with you, perhaps focusing on intention-setting or gratitude. Allow the soothing voice to guide you through the process, helping you visualize your goals and connect with your feelings.

3. Mindful Walking

Meditation can transcend stillness; it can also be active. Mindful walking is an extraordinary way to integrate movement with awareness. Find a quiet space, indoors or outdoors, where you can wander without distractions. As you walk, pay attention to each step—the sensation of your feet touching the ground, the rhythm of your breath, and the sounds around you. Let each step remind you that you are present in this moment. This practice not only calms the mind but also connects you with your body, reinforcing the theme of intentionality.

4. Body Scan Meditation

Lie down in a comfortable position, allowing your body to relax against the surface beneath you. Close your eyes and take a few deep breaths. Begin by directing your attention to your toes, observing any sensations, tension, or relaxation. Gradually expand your awareness, moving from your feet to your head. This practice cultivates a deep connection between mind and body, fostering a clear understanding of your current state. If you notice discomfort or areas requiring attention, breathe into that space, welcoming the sensations without judgment.

These meditation techniques serve as powerful tools for cultivating a mindful approach to life. With consistent practice, they enhance your ability to focus on intentions, foster emotional regulation, and create a spaciousness in which conscious decisions can thrive.

Journaling: The Power of Reflection

Another potent method for cultivating mindfulness is journaling. This practice enables individuals to articulate thoughts and feelings, paving the way for self-exploration and deeper understanding. Through writing, we can clarify intentions, reflect on choices, and visualize aspirations.

1. Morning Pages

Morning Pages, popularized by Julia Cameron in *The Artist's Way*, involves writing three pages of stream-of-consciousness thoughts upon waking, before engaging in daily activities. There is no right or wrong way to write; let your thoughts flow without censorship. The primary objective is to clear your mind of clutter and engage with your innermost feelings. This process often reveals insights about your intentions and the choices you wish to make throughout the day.

2. Intention Journaling

Set aside time each week to reflect on your goals and aspirations. Ask yourself: What do I want to achieve? How do I want to feel? Write down your intentions in vivid detail, imagining yourself experiencing them. Consider the steps you can take to bring these intentions to fruition. This practice fosters clarity and serves as a roadmap for your decisions, keeping your goals front and center.

3. Gratitude Journaling

Gratitude enhances mindfulness by shifting our focus toward abundance. Dedicate a few minutes each day to note at least three things you're grateful for. They could be as simple as a sunny day, a smile from a stranger, or the warmth of your favorite mug. Gratitude journaling reinforces the positive aspects of life and allows you to appreciate the present moment, creating fertile ground for intentional choices.

4. Reflective Journaling

After making an important decision, dedicate time to reflect on the process. What influenced your choice? How did it feel at the moment? What are the consequences of that decision? Use this space to analyze your emotions and thoughts surrounding the choice, gaining insights that improve future decision-making. This reflective approach deepens mindfulness by connecting past experiences to present actions.

Integrating journaling into your routine enhances self-awareness, clarity, and intentionality. It transforms superficial thoughts into profound insights, guiding you on your journey.

Daily Affirmations: Speaking Your Intentions ·

Affirmations are powerful tools for conditioning the mind toward positivity and clarityNashville These statements, spoken or written in the present tense, act as reminders of your intentions and capabilities. By consistently affirming your desires, you align your subconscious mind with your conscious intentions, solidifying your commitment to intentional living.

1. Creating Personal Affirmations

Identify the intentions you wish to embody. Write affirmations that resonate with your goals, framing them in positive, present terms. For example, instead of saying, "I will be confident," frame it as, "I am confident and capable." Repeat these affirmations daily, preferably in the morning, to set the tone for your day. Consider incorporating them into your journaling practice, writing them down as part of your creative process.

2. Visualization Techniques

Alongside affirmations, visualization enhances their effectiveness. Picture yourself embodying the affirmation. What does it feel like? How do you carry yourself? Enhance the imagery by incorporating sensory details—imagine the sights, sounds, and sensations around you. This dual approach strengthens your belief in your ability to achieve your intentions while remaining grounded in present awareness.

3. Affirmation Reminders

Write your affirmations on sticky notes and place them where you will frequently see them—on your bathroom mirror, computer, or refrigerator. This constant visual reminder strengthens mindfulness and commitment to intentional choices. When you see them, pause to recite the affirmations aloud, allowing them to resonate in your mind.

4. Group Affirmation Sessions

Consider creating affirmations with friends or family. Gather periodically to share your intentions and affirmations. This collective energy increases motivation, accountability, and connection. Sharing your aspirations and speaking them aloud can amplify their impact, allowing your intentions to take root in supportive community soil.

As we integrate affirmations into our daily lives, we foster a profound shift in perspective. We learn to replace self-doubt with confidence, amplifying our commitment to living intentionally.

Creating a Mindful Routine

Mindfulness is not a standalone practice; it thrives when integrated into daily routines. Below are suggestions for creating sustainable habits that blend mindfulness with intentionality:

1. Mindful Mornings

Start each day with dedicated time for mindfulness practices. This could involve a combination of meditation, journaling, and affirmations. By committing to this time, you prepare yourself for the day ahead with focus and intention.

271

2. Mindful Commuting

Transform commuting time into an opportunity for mindfulness. Whether driving or using public transport, use this time to practice breathing exercises or listen to guided meditations. Allow the journey to become a sacred ritual, creating a calming transition into and out of your day.

3. Mindful Breaks

Incorporate moments of mindfulness during the day, even if just for a minute or two. Take short breaks to breathe deeply, stretch, or refocus your intentions. These micro-practices can rejuvenate your mind and body, preventing overwhelm and promoting clarity in your choices.

4. Evening Reflections

At the end of each day, reflect on your experiences. What choices did you make? How did they align with your intentions? Use this space to journal your thoughts, noting what went well and areas for growth. This reflective practice reinforces the day's learnings and sets the stage for tomorrow.

By consistently engaging in these practices, mindfulness transcends moments and becomes a lifestyle. The blessings of being intentional grow as we embrace clarity and purposefulness in our choices, steering us toward more enriched lives.

Conclusion

Cultivating mindfulness is an ongoing journey, inviting us to explore, reflect, and grow. Through meditation, journaling, and daily affirmations, we unlock the potential for greater awareness and deliberate living. As we engage in these practices, we center ourselves in the present moment, aligning our choices with our intentions.

Ultimately, the beauty of mindfulness lies in its ability to connect us with ourselves and the world around us. By intentionally infusing our lives with these practices, we foster resilience, clarity, and a profound sense of gratitude for every moment we experience. As we become more present, our choices resonate beyond the surface, shaping our futures and guiding our paths with purpose and love.

Choosing Your Own Adventure

The Adventure of Life

Life is an adventure, a beautifully intricate tapestry woven with choices, experiences, and unwritten stories that unfold along the way. Each moment presents an opportunity to step beyond the mundane, to view our existence not merely as a series of tasks and responsibilities but as an expansive journey brimming with potential. Imagine standing at the edge of a vast wilderness, where every fork in the trail beckons with the promise of discovery, where the peaks of mountains and the depths of valleys await your exploration. It is here that we understand that life is far more than mere survival; it is an invitation to venture forth, to uncover the treasures hidden within each choice we make.

As children, we approach the world with eyes wide open, eager to touch, taste, and experience everything life offers. That innate wonder—the thrill of building a fort from pillows, the rush of swinging higher than the treetops, or the joy of making friends on a playground—sets the stage for our understanding of adventure. In those moments, our choices feel boundless, as if each decision opens another door to happiness and curiosity. Somewhere along the path to adulthood, we often forget this fundamental truth. The weight of expectations, responsibilities, and societal norms can cloud our vision, transforming an exhilarating journey into a checklist of daily tasks. Yet, the essence of adventure lies within us, patiently waiting to be rediscovered.

Let us embark on a quest through the metaphorical landscapes of life, where each decision leads to new territories. Picture the adventure as a sprawling forest, rich with vibrant flora and fauna, where the air is thick with the scent of possibility. Each tree stands as a choice, its branches stretching outward to signify the many directions our lives can take. The journey through this forest is not always easy; it is full of thickets and brambles that test our path. Yet, those obstacles shape our character, testing our courage and resolve.

In this enchanted forest, every choice carries the weight of both risk and reward. Picture a wise old tree, its gnarled roots deeply embedded in the earth, offering counsel to those brave enough to seek its shade. "To choose is to venture into the unknown," it might say. "Each path you take leads to new experiences, but the beauty lies not only in the destination but in the journey itself." As we listen to this ancient wisdom, we entertain the idea that our lives are not scripted but rather improvised performances, each act revealing a new layer of ourselves as we navigate the unfolding narrative.

Consider the tale of a young traveler named Alex. With a heart full of dreams and a spirit hungry for exploration, Alex ventured into the unknown after high school, leaving behind the familiar comforts of home. The decision to explore life beyond their small town was the first transformative step in a journey filled with exhilarating and challenging adventures. Alex's initial decision was to take a gap year, filled with choices—from backpacking through foreign countries and volunteering in communities to learning new languages and cultures.

Amid the myriad choices, there were moments of doubt. Standing on the brink of a cliff overlooking the shimmering expanse of the sea, Alex hesitated. The jump into the water below symbolized more than a physical leap; it represented a commitment to embracing the unknown, to surrendering to the currents of life instead of always steering the boat. At that moment, everything felt suspended in time, and the whisper of adventure urged Alex to take the plunge. With a deep breath, propelled by the rush of possibilities, they leapt into the water, a surge of adrenaline and exhilaration flooding their senses. The water enveloped them, turning the fear of the unknown into euphoria as they emerged laughing and breathless, ready for whatever lay ahead.

The beauty of adventure often lies in the unexpected detours we encounter. Just as nature surprises us with hidden valleys and sparkling springs, life presents opportunities cloaked as obstacles. During a spontaneous trek in a remote village, Alex found themselves lost. The map failed to indicate the winding mountain trails, and frustration threatened to overshadow the thrill of exploration. Yet, as the sun dipped below the horizon, bathing the landscape in shades of orange and gold, Alex realized that being lost was a journey of its own. Instead of panic, curiosity bloomed; they turned the misstep into an exploration of beauty, encountering friendly locals and uncharted views that would not have been part of the intended route.

With each experience, Alex not only collected stories but also forged an identity molded by choice. Each interaction with people from different cultures, each challenge faced without a safety net, and each moment immersed in natural wonders expanded their horizons and understanding of life's vastness. It was as if Alex was filling a canvas with bright colors and bold strokes, creating a masterpiece with every decision, fueled by the understanding that adventure is not an endpoint but a continual process of evolution and discovery.

Yet, as the adventure of life unfolds, we must not shy away from the lessons learned in moments of discomfort. Every adventure has its trials. There will be treacherous paths, steep climbs, and dark nights where fear seeps in, casting shadows over our aspirations. It is during these times that we discover who we are. Every misadventure prepares us for the next, adding depth to the story we craft. Alex encountered setbacks—currency theft in a bustling city, a missed flight that led to nights spent in an airport, and friendships that didn't blossom as hoped. Each incident, while seemingly negative, became an opportunity for growth, resilience, and new lessons.

Instead of allowing fear of failure to inhibit further adventures, Alex learned to embrace these moments as integral parts of the expedition. Each failure transformed into a stepping stone, leading to greater clarity and determination. Learning a new language after misunderstanding directions became a source of humor and connection with those around them. Making mistakes became a strategy for cultivating empathy and understanding toward others, enriching their travel experiences and expanding their worldview.

As we traverse this adventure of life, each chapter filled with choices embellishes our narrative, weaving a rich tapestry of experiences. Vivid storytelling amplifies the thrill of every decision, as if we were flipping through the pages of an enchanting storybook. Each decision spirals into new narratives, breathing life into the essence of our existence. Each encounter is a new character, each journey a new chapter, populated with lessons learned.

Let's pause and reflect on how our lives mirror this adventure. The beauty of choice lies within our hands, just as we wield a brush to create on a blank canvas. What colors will we choose? Will our bold strokes reflect vibrant hues of joy and adventure, or will we stick to subdued colors of fear and conformity? The adventure lies not in escaping challenges but in welcoming them, dancing with the winds of change as we navigate both calm and stormy seas.

As we recommit to our paths of adventure, let us envision ourselves scaling the heights of our potential, journeying through life with open hearts and curious minds. At every decision point, pause, examine the landscape before us, and ask:

- What new territories am I ready to explore?

- What fears am I willing to acknowledge and overcome?

- How can I transform the ordinary into the extraordinary?

In embracing an adventure mindset, we place more value on the process of living than on outcomes. Life is dynamic— a constant ebb and flow between heart and mind, action and reflection. The journey transforms us, shapes us, and guides us back to the true pulse of existence.

At the heart of every great adventure lies community. Just as Alex forged connections with fellow travelers, we can find strength in the communities we build through our choices. We do not navigate the adventure of life in isolation; we are surrounded by fellow adventurers, each carving their own path while contributing to a shared experience.

The friendships we cultivate serve as anchors, guiding us back to what matters as we work through the trials and tribulations of our search for meaning. Adventure is not merely a solitary endeavor; it is a collective experience, weaving diverse narratives into a vibrant tapestry. As we embark on our journeys, we are urged to take these connections seriously, to nurture and cultivate them as companions through which we share our joys, fears, and lessons learned.

Let us not forget that every great adventure culminates in moments of reflection. Just as Alex journaled their journeys—capturing the vivid emotions of exhilaration, fear, joy, and insight—so too must we reflect on our adventures. This contemplation develops a deeper understanding of how far we've come and what lies ahead, allowing us to pause and appreciate the beauty of the moments that make up our unique stories. As we reflect, we distill our experiences into lessons; we extract meaning from the paths that brought us joy and navigate what choices may offer the twists and turns needed for future exploration.

The beauty of our adventure lies in the promise that it is ongoing, that every ending is a new beginning. Our lives are filled with infinite potential. Just as Alex continued to travel beyond the initial year of exploration, we can embrace the reality that our journeys have no expiration date. This invites us to approach every day as a fresh page, ripe for our creations, choices, and adventures.

As we draw this journey toward its conclusion, let us bask in the glow of our adventure. Let us leave behind the notion of mere survival and embrace the richness of life that unfolds through choosing. Each leap into the unknown, each decision made with intention, composes the melody of our existence, creating a vibrant symphony that resonates through the corridors of time.

In closing, remember that life is the grandest of adventures, beckoning with open arms for those who embrace its uncertainty. The mountains may be steep, and the valleys deep, but within them lies the heart of authenticity, experience, and connection. Each choice invites exploration, excitement, and discovery—an adventure that cannot be scripted, only lived vibrantly and boldly. So, step forth. Dare to choose. The adventure awaits.

Creating Your Path

As we journey through life, we navigate a landscape rich with possibilities. Each decision, no matter how small, contributes to the vibrant tapestry of our existence, shaping our experiences and defining who we are. The essence of living an intentional life lies in recognizing that we are not mere bystanders; we are the authors of our own adventure stories. Creating your path is not just about selecting a direction; it is about actively engaging in writing your life's narrative.

To begin this journey, let's embrace the idea that daily choices hold immense potential to alter our lives' course. Whether contemplating a career change, exploring new relationships, or defining passions and interests, the possibilities for our stories are endless. The world is a canvas, and we are the artists. Each of us has a unique palette of colors to express our individuality and dreams, inviting creativity into our goal-setting.

Becoming an Active Participant

To understand the significance of being an active participant in your life story, consider the metaphor of a travel agent. Imagine planning a trip without expressing your preferences;

it would lead to a journey devoid of personal meaning. In contrast, when you take charge of planning your excursion, you choose destinations, create an itinerary, and select activities that excite you. The same principle applies to life. By actively participating in decision-making, you craft an adventure that reflects your aspirations and values.

Action is essential in turning aspirations into reality. Just as a travel agent needs to know travel routes, costs, and accommodations, you must equip yourself with self-awareness and understand what matters most to you. This requires deep reflection on your values, passions, and desires. Start by asking pivotal questions:

- What do I love to do, and what brings me genuine joy?

- What are my core values, and how do they influence my decisions?

- What experiences do I want that would shape my life narrative positively?

Once you have these answers, visioning becomes more focused. Start defining your adventure in tangible terms.

Mapping Out Your Desired Adventure

Creating your path involves systematically mapping out your

goals and the adventures you wish to undertake. Picture this process as plotting a treasure map. The 'X' marks the spot where your dreams lie. Your mission is to navigate potential obstacles and challenges while remaining aware of opportunities ahead.

Utilizing a visual representation of your goals can energize this process. Consider creating a vision board—a collage or digital layout combining words, images, and quotes to represent what you want to achieve. Here's how to create one:

1. **Gather Materials**: Collect magazines, photographs, and craft supplies or use digital tools like Canva or Pinterest.

2. **Identify Your Aspirations**: Reflect on your desires and goals. What do you want to accomplish in the upcoming year or over the next five years?

3. **Select Images and Words**: Look for visuals that resonate with your aspirations. Choose images and phrases that encapsulate the feelings or achievements you wish to attract.

4. **Assemble Your Board**: Arrange your chosen visuals on your board. There is no right or wrong way; it's about what feels right for you.

5. **Display It Prominently**: Place your vision board where you will see it regularly, serving as a daily reminder of your objectives and dreams.

Your vision board acts as a dynamic representation of your goals, but creating it is only the beginning. Regularly engage with it to ensure aspirations remain alive in your consciousness. Reflect on your feelings about the images and words chosen. Are they still relevant? Do you need to update or add new aspirations? Allow your vision board to evolve as you grow.

Inviting Creativity into Goal-Setting

Once you have a visual representation of your goals, engage creativity in the goal-setting process. Goals do not have to be rigid or limiting; they can be fluid, exciting, and bold. Transform your goals into creative expressions with these exercises:

- **Artistic Journaling**: Use a notebook to blend traditional journaling with artistic endeavors. Incorporate sketches, doodles, or collages related to your goals. Writing and drawing stimulate different parts of the brain and can lead to inspiration you may not have considered.

- **Storyboarding**: Sketch key events you envision on your journey. Create a storyboard where each panel represents a significant step toward your goal. Describe how you will feel as you achieve each segment, making it vivid and engaging in your mind.

- **Goal Parables**: Write short stories or parables representing your goals and aspirations. Frame them as tales of characters embarking on transformative journeys, mirroring your own. You'll find depth in storytelling as you illustrate hurdles and triumphs.

- **Mind Mapping**: Use a mind map to explore your goals visually. Begin with a central idea, branching out into categories encompassing your aspirations. The freedom of a mind map can unveil connections you may not have recognized.

Engaging with goals creatively taps into emotions and insights that may not emerge from rigid planning. It empowers you to find joy in the process rather than viewing goals as mere checklists.

The Exhilaration of Shaping Your Narrative

The adventure of life is inherently exhilarating, filled with the unknown, the unexpected, and the profound. When you take the reins and shape your narrative, you invite excitement into each day. Understand that this journey may come with uncertainties and challenges, yet these elements are crucial to growth and transformation.

Rather than fearing the unknown, shift your perspective to embrace it. Reflect on moments that surprised you most. These often become cherished memories, shaping who you are and offering insights into your character and resilience.

Identify instances where the unexpected led to personal growth. Were there moments you initially resisted but later found pivotal? Use these memories to strengthen your resolve for future choices. Assure yourself that, even if the road ahead is unclear, you have the inner strength to navigate it successfully.

To highlight the importance of shaping your story, consider adaptability. Like a skilled adventurer adjusting their course based on terrain, be willing to pivot in response to new information or experiences. Celebrate adaptability as an asset that allows you to thrive through uncertainties while moving toward your goals.

Conclusion: Your Adventure Awaits

As you embark on creating your path, remember that you hold the power to shape your life with every decision. Embrace your role as the author of your adventure story, richly coloring your journey with curiosity, creativity, and courage. Map out desired adventures through creative exercises, and let your imagination run wild as you set goals aligned with your true self.

We explored becoming an active participant in your life journey, mapping out adventures through creative exercises, and embracing the exhilaration of crafting your unique narrative.

Now is the time to act. Define your first step toward creating your path. What small action can you take today? Whether starting a vision board, writing a page of your story, or envisioning the first chapter of your journey, let it be a commitment to yourself. Your adventure awaits, and it is one only you can create.

Finding Joy Amidst the Journey

As we traverse the winding paths of life, it is essential to appreciate the joy nestled within each choice we make. Too often, the lens through which we view decisions is clouded by expectations, doubts, and echoes of regret. However, within the complex web of decision-making lies a powerful truth: joy can be found amid every twist and turn, often shining brighter during our most unpredictable adventures.

To begin our exploration of joy, acknowledge the foundation for a fulfilling life—gratitude. Gratitude is a transformative practice, a conscious choice to recognize and appreciate the experiences that shape us. Each decision, no matter how small, carries the potential for joy. It reminds us that life is not solely defined by monumental moments but by an accumulation of small victories deserving recognition and celebration.

Embracing our journeys requires shifting focus from perceived failures to viewing each step as a building block in our narratives. A child takes their first step with excitement and trepidation, fueled by the joy of discovery. In that moment of triumph, the world becomes a stage where adventure begins. In this spirit, we can rekindle our joy.

Consider the daily choices we face, from what to eat for breakfast to the path we take on our morning commute. While these may seem mundane, there is hidden joy in consciously choosing what resonates with us—a warm cup of coffee, the soothing embrace of a favorite sweater, or the sound of a favorite song. Each decision is an opportunity to immerse ourselves in life's richness. Pausing to appreciate these moments, we take note of our evolving narrative and the joy embedded within.

Joy extends beyond surface-level choices; it is also born from significant decisions—those that place us at a crossroads. Perhaps it's a career change igniting fear and excitement or a decision to nurture a budding relationship. These pivotal moments weigh heavily, yet they open doors to new possibilities. Joy often mingles with uncertainty, and we must learn to embrace both.

Imagine standing before a fork in the road, all paths equally valid yet diverging. As you contemplate your route, fear may whisper doubts, but within your heart, the spark of joy invites you to leap into the unknown. Choosing is a source of liberation, breathing life into aspirations. Stepping into possibility, we cultivate a deeper understanding of what brings joy.

Small victories measure progress along our journey. They may arrive as unexpected laughter with loved ones, a completed task once daunting, or the quiet satisfaction of self-reflection after a challenging day. These accomplishments foster an environment where joy flourishes. Keeping a gratitude journal can highlight these victories, allowing us to see how far we've come. Each day, jot down three things that brought joy—simple things like a warm sunrise, a meaningful conversation, or the delight of a good book. This practice illuminates life's richness as we celebrate each step, no matter how small.

Yet, joy is often woven into our most unpredictable adventures. Life has an uncanny ability to surprise us, throwing curveballs that may feel daunting but lead to unforeseen delights. Take Clara, a young woman who set out on a cavalcade of adventures to travel the world alone. With minimal savings and a heart full of dreams, she departed for destinations that shifted her perspective and opened her heart.

In one instance, Clara's flight was canceled, leaving her stranded in a foreign city she hadn't planned to visit. Initially overcome with dread, anger, and frustration, she felt at fate's mercy. However, as she wandered the vibrant streets, she stumbled upon a local festival filled with music, dance, and culinary delights. In that moment of serendipity, joy bloomed as she danced with strangers, tasted exotic flavors, and forged connections that would last a lifetime. What was perceived as a setback transformed into an unforgettable memory—a testament to the joy in life's unpredictability.

Every journey offers lessons that teach us to find joy in the unexpected. These moments encourage relinquishing rigid expectations and embracing spontaneity's beauty. A road trip, for instance, often leads to unplanned stops—a scenic overlook, a quirky roadside diner, or a chance encounter with a fellow traveler. These experiences dance with surprise, breaking monotony and reminding us that joy resides outside comfort zones.

Consider your daily choices: How often do you let anticipated outcomes dictate your experience? By shifting to a mindset of openness and curiosity, you open windows of possibility, inviting joy to cascade into your life. Each morning, let your first choice be appreciation. Acknowledge that each day holds potential for joyful experiences. Embracing this mindset, we approach adventures with wide-eyed wonder, sparking joy within.

Our desire for adventure beckons us to forge ahead, with excitement reminiscent of childhood exploration. The world is a canvas waiting to be painted with our experiences, and each brushstroke offers a chance to infuse narratives with joy and appreciation. Being present opens our eyes to moments that might go unnoticed.

When reflecting on choices and experiences, remember to take stock of your path. Consider the metaphor of an artist examining their canvas. With every choice, we add a layer to our narrative. While some layers may be darker, overshadowed by fear or uncertainty, they are equally important in creating the final masterpiece. Acknowledging the full spectrum of experiences honors our journey.

Establishing meaningful rituals can anchor joy in everyday life. Engage in practices that prompt reflection, whether through meditation, storytelling with loved ones, or time in nature. Allow life's rhythm to grace your senses—the warm sunlight during a walk, the calming sound of raindrops, or laughter shared in a cozy gathering.

By paying attention to these experiences, we become participants rather than observers. Finding joy requires cultivating presence and appreciation. Create rituals that remind you to celebrate life's ebb and flow.

As we savor experiences, we weave a narrative reflecting who we are. Align choices with core values, for they serve as a compass directing our adventures. Like a journey through a forest, trials may be steep, yet clarity of purpose softens them, allowing joy to flourish even in challenging circumstances.

Finding joy also requires vulnerability. Engaging authentically opens us to risks that may seem intimidating. Sharing stories, exposing our hearts, and embracing imperfections create connections that deepen our experience and foster joy.

Consider those who inspire joy through authenticity, creating movements that connect people globally. Through vulnerability, joy is cultivated within and among those beside us. Every shared story invites reflection, empathy, and joy beyond the individual.

In your life, note those who radiate positivity, lifting your spirits and reminding you of the light within life's adventures. As we journey together, we empower one another to own our stories, celebrating every choice and experience.

As we conclude our exploration of joy amidst the journey, remember that adventure lies in our choices—the bold and timid, easy and complicated. It is a call to embrace every moment, cultivating gratitude for small victories while growing from life's unpredictability. Joy is not a destination but a vibrant companion, cheering us as we navigate existence's landscapes.

In closing, find the courage to embark on your adventures, cherishing choices that shape your path. Celebrate the joy within every step, for within this journey lies the essence of living.

Every choice is an opportunity for discovery, a chance for joy to illuminate your days. As you step into your story, embrace its unpredictability, and let joy seep into your being. The tapestry of your life is rich with experiences waiting to be lived, painted with the colors of choice and adventure. So go forth, and may your quest for joy continue with every choice you make.

The Legacy of Choice

Beyond the Present

In quiet moments of reflection, one cannot help but feel the weight of choices made. Each decision is akin to a ripple in a vast pond, sending waves outward, affecting not only our lives but also weaving through the fabric of generations to come. The choices made today are not merely immediate actions; they are threads that shape the story of our lives, our families, and, ultimately, humanity.

To consider our choices in this manner shifts the paradigm

of decision-making from a transient act to a profound act of creation. It poses challenging questions: What legacy am I leaving with my choices? How will they echo through the lives of my children, their children, and beyond? Every choice has the potential for monumental impact, and when viewed through this lens, the notion of choice evolves into a sacred responsibility.

Consider the individual who chooses a profession not just for personal gain but with an understanding of its societal implications. A teacher dedicates years to shaping minds, fostering a love for learning that can inspire generations. The knowledge and values imparted in the classroom do not end with one group of students; they cascade forward, influencing how those students interact with the world, impacting their future families, and affecting countless lives. This is the true nature of legacy—small actions leading to massive transformations.

The stories of remarkable individuals often emerge from seemingly small choices. For instance, consider Rosa Parks, who refused to give up her seat—an action bold in its simplicity. This choice became a catalyst for the civil rights movement, igniting a flame that inspired others to challenge injustice. Her act of defiance transcended time, becoming a

298

luminous marker on the timeline of social justice, reshaping societal norms and challenging oppressive systems.

Conversely, there are choices made in silence, often overlooked but equally impactful. A parent's choice to express love and acceptance can resonate through generations, breaking cycles of hurt and fostering a culture of understanding. Consider a small-town farmer who adopts sustainable farming practices. By prioritizing the health of the land, they not only improve yields but also leave a more fertile world for future generations. Within this sphere of influence, the interconnectedness of choice and legacy becomes strikingly evident.

Through these narratives, we find that the implications of our choices stretch far beyond personal ambition or satisfaction. They intertwine with the essence of community and shared humanity. The cause and effect of a single choice can rally communities, inspire movements, or initiate healing. History is rife with examples where one person's decision propelled the collective toward a progressive or regressive path.

Looking beyond our personal sphere, let's focus on the collective responsibility we share as members of society. Each time we choose compassion over apathy, understanding over judgment, or action over inaction, we contribute to a culture of empathy that lays a sturdy foundation for future generations. This fosters an environment where love, kindness, and justice not only exist but thrive. We might ask ourselves: What message do we want to pass down? A legacy of love or one of fear?

A community leader who invests in educational programs for underprivileged youth shapes not just the lives of the current cohort but also the futures of countless descendants. The impact is exponential, as these youths become positive catalysts in their communities. They are not merely beneficiaries of opportunities but contributors to a chain reaction that inspires further change. This is a living testament to the power of choice—the ability to intentionally mold futures and create ripples that touch lives in ways we may never see.

Engagement in the civic arena is another poignant avenue through which choices manifest legacy. Individuals who take a stand on pressing issues—be it climate change, healthcare, education, or equality—shine a spotlight on societal currents. Grassroots movements often begin with a few passionate voices who choose to challenge the status quo. These acts of courage foster a collective consciousness and present a call to action that can influence policy, reform societal attitudes, and inspire future leaders to continue the work.

Rewinding history, we observe pivotal choices made during transformative periods. The Founding Fathers of the United States chose to birth a nation on the principles of liberty and equality. Their decisions, rooted in vision, profoundly affected their contemporaries and charted a course for principles that resonate globally, influencing future generations in their pursuits of justice and freedom.

As we acknowledge this continuum, a poignant realization emerges: the dangers of choices made in silence. Choosing to ignore social wrongs or remain complicit in the face of injustice can perpetuate cycles of harm and create legacies steeped in resentment and division. History's heavy lessons reveal that inaction, indifference, and fear also articulate a legacy, often breeding negative outcomes. This awareness underscores the importance of mindful decision-making, pressing upon us an urgent responsibility to weigh our choices against their collective impact.

The concept of legacy, however, does not solely encompass dramatic changes or grand gestures. Often, the most profound legacies are those of everyday kindness and compassion. A mentor who invests time in their protégés shapes the foundation for future leaders, fostering a culture of support and growth. A neighbor who lends a helping hand during hard times strengthens the fabric of interconnectedness, reinforcing values of generosity and camaraderie. These choices, integral to community life, create narratives of resilience that characterize the lineage of social and familial legacies, imparting wisdom on service and altruism.

Imagine sitting around a dinner table, generations represented, each voice contributing to the collective family legacy. Through stories passed down, we recognize how values, norms, and practices are carried from one generation to the next. This intergenerational transmission relies heavily on conscious choice; the choices made today shape the stories told tomorrow. This speaks to the heart of legacy: What aspects of our lives do we wish to be remembered? What stories do we want our children and their children to carry forward?

Reflecting on one's choices is inherently introspective, a journey that can be complex and challenging. It requires honesty, vulnerability, and a willingness to confront uncomfortable truths. Each individual must grapple with the question: How do my choices today reflect my values and aspirations for future generations? In an age of technology and rapid change, this consideration becomes even more essential. Digital footprints and social media interactions carry the potential to shape narratives that persist long after we are gone.

Each generation faces unique challenges and opportunities, yet an underlying truth connects us: choices made in clarity can pave the way for progress, while those made in haste can lead to unforeseen consequences. The responsibility lies within each of us to engage with our decisions constructively, for our actions today compose the soundtrack of tomorrow's legacy. This requires a commitment to conscious living— being present, aware, and intentional in our choices.

Empowered by awareness, individuals can turn small actions into profound legacies. A person who volunteers at a local shelter ignites a chain of goodwill that spirals into the community. Those touched by kindness often pay it forward, creating an environment rich with compassion and solidarity. This can lead to community movements that transform not just individual lives but entire neighborhoods.

Yet, as we delve into this intricate web of choice and legacy, the fear of responsibility may loom large. How can one person make a difference in the face of such vastness? It is essential to recognize that monumental change is not a solitary effort. Each small step contributes to a larger march forward; every choice, no matter how minute, holds significance. Just as a single candle can illuminate a dark room, individual decisions light a collective path toward a hopeful future.

Embracing this responsibility fosters resilience in the face of adversity. Those facing challenges often find their greatest strength in the choices they make—even when confronting fears, doubts, and uncertainties. The narrative becomes one of strength rooted in decisions that prioritize kindness, justice, and authenticity, planting seeds for future generations who will face their own battles. In doing so, we equip future generations with a legacy that can withstand storms—a testament to the power of hope.

Ultimately, the choices that define our lives also shape our legacy. They carve out a space in history, influencing landscapes from neighborhoods to nations. As we become aware of the weight our choices carry, it becomes clear: we are not just crafting our narratives; we are weaving threads into the grand tapestry of humanity.

As we conclude our reflections, let us commit to a pledge—to choose consciously, act with intention, and foster awareness of the profound implications our choices hold. Let us choose joy, kindness, and love, knowing that each choice lays down a story for future generations—a story of resilience, hope, and faith in the goodness of humanity. The legacies we create will reverberate through time, providing light and guidance to those who walk the paths we leave behind.

What will you choose today? How will you shape the future with every action and decision? Each choice, each moment of sincerity or fearlessness, given intention, can lead to a legacy that your descendants will cherish, learn from, and carry forward. Let each heartbeat remind you that it is not only about today but about those who will rise because of the choices we make. Embrace the responsibility of your choices, for the future is in your hands.

Passing the Torch of Empowerment

The act of choosing is not merely a personal endeavor; it reverberates through the lives of those around us, shaping their experiences, aspirations, and identities. Every decision holds the potential to empower or diminish, to inspire or deter. As we understand this interconnectedness, we realize that our choices extend beyond our individual lives and touch the fabric of our communities, especially influencing younger generations who look to us as role models, mentors, and guides.

Our choices communicate a powerful message, whether intentional or not. They serve as a mirror reflecting our values, priorities, and beliefs. This reflective nature is particularly potent for children and young adults; they observe, absorb, and emulate the actions of adults in their lives. Each time we choose kindness, resilience, and integrity, we send a message of empowerment to young minds. Conversely, when we succumb to fear or negativity, we may inadvertently instill doubt and apprehension in those who look up to us.

This journey toward understanding the weight of our choices has a crucial component: the mindset we cultivate within ourselves and share with others. By fostering a culture of intentionality, we create an environment that values mindful decision-making. When we approach choices deliberately—aware of implications and consequences—we set an example for others to follow.

In a world filled with distractions and external pressures, intentional living is a radical choice. It encourages us to step back, reflect on what matters, and align actions with core values. For young people navigating complex social landscapes, witnessing adults practice intentional thinking illuminates their decision-making processes, helping them cultivate critical thinking and self-awareness.

The Importance of Role Modeling

Sharing our experiences, both victories and failures, empowers those around us. The stories we tell—about overcoming obstacles, making tough choices, or learning from mistakes—inspire reflection in others. This is particularly true for adolescents and young adults searching for their identities and place in the world. Such conversations unfold like a tapestry, where threads of wisdom weave together, forming a collective narrative of empowerment and resilience.

Consider a young person who watches a mentor pursue their dreams despite setbacks. They see perseverance, adaptation, and growth. This experience plants seeds of courage and motivation, guiding them toward daring choices in their own lives. Such moments solidify the understanding that every choice carries weight, that they, too, can embrace the power to decide their paths.

Cultivating Mindful Choices

To ensure our choices communicate empowering messages, we must practice mindfulness in decision-making. Being present means slowing down to consider short- and long-term consequences. This approach invites probing questions:

- What values am I embodying through this choice?

- How will this decision impact those around me?

- Does this align with the legacy I wish to leave?

By engaging with these questions, we transform decision-making from reactive habits into thoughtful actions. This intentional practice empowers ourselves and those watching us, becoming part of our legacy by modeling a way of living that prioritizes reflection, adaptability, and purpose.

The Ripple Effect

Every choice sends ripples through our communities. Imagine a stone dropped into still water—each ripple represents the far-reaching impact of our actions. Young individuals may not immediately grasp the depth of these ripples, but as they grow, they recognize the legacy formed through our decisions.

For instance, a teacher who creates a supportive, inclusive

classroom empowers students to feel confident sharing their thoughts and ideas. As these students enter their own spheres of influence, they carry this empowerment forward, creating similar environments of support and acceptance in their workplaces.

Reflective Exercises for Legacy Building

Encouraging reflection on the legacy we wish to pass on requires structured exercises. Here are prompts to assist in this discovery:

1. **Personal Values Assessment**: List the core values that define you. How do these translate into daily choices? Are there instances where you acted contrary to these values? Reflect on how to align future choices with your principles.

2. **Legacy Visualization**: Visualize how you want to be remembered. What impact do you wish to have on those around you? Write a letter to your future self, outlining the legacy you want to cultivate. Revisit it yearly to assess growth.

3. **Mentorship Mapping**: Identify individuals you want to influence positively. How can you model choices

that empower them? Outline specific actions or decisions to provide support, guidance, or encouragement.

4. **Empowerment Moments**: Recall a time when someone's choices inspired or empowered you. What did they do, and how did it change your perspective? Document how you can replicate similar actions.

5. **Accountability Partner Exercise**: Engage with a trusted friend or family member to discuss legacy aspirations. Create an accountability plan, identifying choices and behaviors to work on. Check in regularly to assess progress and reinforce changes.

Inspiring Future Generations

To pass the torch of empowerment, we must create platforms for young people to express themselves—forums for dialogue, opportunity, and connection. These can include community service projects, mentorship programs, or workshops focused on skill-building and self-discovery.

Encouraging young people to participate in decision-making processes affecting their lives fosters agency and responsibility. Understanding that their choices matter empowers them to influence outcomes, transforming their perspective.

Instilling a growth mindset in the younger generation encourages viewing challenges as opportunities for learning. This resilience empowers them to make bold choices and cultivates confidence to carve their own paths, even in adversity.

A Call for Responsibility

Empowerment comes with responsibility. Every choice can uplift or hinder. As stewards of our legacy, we must commit to choices reflecting compassion, openness, and honesty. This means learning, accepting feedback, and growing alongside the younger generations we empower.

This commitment ripples out, influencing the next generation to approach decisions with mindfulness and intention. We inspire a culture of compassionate decision-making, driven by the understanding that every choice contributes to a larger narrative of collective empowerment.

Changing the Narrative

Society often cultivates a narrative of competition, scarcity, and fear. Counteracting this involves embracing abundance—seeing possibilities and creating a culture that celebrates collaboration and support. Every empowering choice chips away at this narrative, replacing it with one that uplifts and inspires.

Approaching decisions from abundance and empowerment demonstrates that we can choose a path fostering growth, inclusivity, and resilience. We remove boundaries from dreams, cultivating environments where individuals feel capable of achieving their potential.

The Legacy of Love

At the heart of passing the torch is love—the love we extend to ourselves and others. Love becomes a guiding force behind choices. Choosing love uplifts, inspires, and empowers. Acknowledging every individual's worth lays the groundwork for a legacy of appreciation. When the younger generation feels valued, they embrace their power to choose with confidence.

The Shared Journey

Passing the torch of empowerment is a shared journey, where every choice builds upon those before it. As we empower others, we create space for collective learning and growth. This reciprocal process reminds us that, though we lead, empowerment is mutual.

Let us be intentional in our choices, mindful of the legacies we create, and courageous in empowering future generations. Through our decisions, we can craft a narrative of strength, resilience, and possibility—a legacy of hope that transcends time.

An Invitation to Reflect

As we conclude this exploration, consider this an invitation to ongoing reflection. What legacy do you wish to pass on? How can your choices contribute to empowering those around you?

This reflection offers an opportunity to become an active creator of change. Let us choose intentionally, inspire with love, and pass the torch of empowerment courageously to the generations that follow.

Future Generations

As we stand at the intersection of our individual lives and the broader tapestry of humanity, we realize the profound impact of our choices, not just on our paths but on the trajectories of future generations. Every decision, no matter how small, stitches itself into the fabric of our family history and cultural heritage. Like a continuous thread, these choices weave through time, impacting lives we may never meet, creating echoes that resonate for years to come.

Our lives are like a forest, with branches extending into infinity. Each branch represents potential lives shaped by our choices today. We may not always consider how our actions influence the future; however, recognizing the weight these decisions carry is imperative. When we understand our role in a larger story—one including ancestors, peers, and descendants—we gain a new perspective on accountability and responsibility.

Imagine a mother facing adversity who pursues education despite challenges. Each late-night study session and tear shed in frustration is a choice toward a better future. Years later, her children observe this resilience, learning the value of education and perseverance. As they navigate their paths, they carry inherited strength, a thread woven into their beings because of their mother's choices. This narrative of hope continues as new generations emerge, fueled by lessons of courage.

The idea of choice extends beyond individual decisions to collective ones made as communities. When families, neighborhoods, or cultures choose kindness over cruelty or collaboration over division, the impact can shift paradigms. These ripples can redefine societal norms and expectations. Collective choices intertwine, forming a bond that nurtures positive growth into the future.

In contrast, we must reflect on choices leading to negative consequences. A community ignoring environmental issues for short-term gains may result in pollution, degradation, and climate change that future generations will bear. These decisions remind us that neglecting responsibility amplifies consequences, forcing descendants to contend with burdens not their own.

As we navigate life, we must decide consciously for ourselves and those who follow. The light of our choices should illuminate paths for others, guiding them toward self-discovery, purpose, and potential. In this light, hope flourishes—a hope grounded in the belief that today's choices can lead to an empowered, wise, and empathetic future.

Embracing this legacy requires reflecting on our ancestors' stories and histories. We inherit a history of triumphs and tribulations shaped by their choices. These lessons provide insights for navigating our journeys. Acknowledging our ancestors' hardships and victories ensures our stories impart knowledge and strength to those who follow.

As we consider our legacy, we face difficult questions: What will our children learn from us? How will our choices shape their views? What story are we telling through our actions?

The narrative we construct today molds the character of future generations. Legacy is built through continual reflection, acting consciously in pursuit of the best outcomes for ourselves and others. This conscientiousness perpetuates values, beliefs, and ideals we hold dear.

To create a legacy resonating positively, we must prioritize intentionality in daily life. Leading with purpose empowers our descendants to choose from knowledge, understanding their connection to the past while owning their futures. Encouraging dialogue and fostering environments where youth express themselves creates a nurturing space for exploring ideas and identities.

Personal development is also crucial. Our growth equips us to guide the next generation. Seeking improvement—through education, self-reflection, or new cultures—expands our perspectives, allowing us to lead by example.

The power of collective choices becomes evident when paired with this realization. Each generation faces unique challenges, but shared knowledge mitigates burdens. Building communities rooted in love, respect, and understanding forges a path uplifting everyone. When the collective recognizes its power, outcomes can be extraordinary, with future generations inheriting a legacy of unity and compassion.

As we explore these interconnections, we ask how our legacy can bridge generational gaps. This requires humility to understand history and courage to change the narrative where necessary. Recognizing where ancestors faltered allows us to correct, learn, and grow beyond past mistakes, sending a message of progress to those who follow—one encouraging boundary-pushing, calculated risks, and authenticity.

Reflecting on our past and present prepares us for the future. The legacies we create become the backdrop for future generations, shaping their identities and choices. Though daunting, embracing this truth lends clarity and purpose. As we grapple with the world's realities, the power of choice remains a divine gift, passed through generations—a legacy inspiring hope in dark times.

In uncertainty, cultivating possibility in all we do is vital. Every decision can contribute to a vibrant, affirming world for those who follow. We are not merely leaving memories; we are offering insights, love, and pathways toward a brighter future. Let us envision what we want for the next generation.

For every choice, consider its effects a decade, a century, or a millennium from now. Will our choices create a world of empathy, compassion, and collaboration? Or perpetuate division and stagnation? This lens ignites urgency in aligning actions with values, reinforcing intentionality. While we cannot control every outcome, we can harness the gift of choice.

The narrative of our futures is collectively written. One person's decisions become the foundation for others, creating momentum inspiring communities, societies, and nations. Schools of thought once silenced may find voices restored through today's choices, leading future generations to enrich and expand upon their inheritance. This cycle of inquiry and growth becomes a legacy worth celebrating.

As we forge ahead, let compassion guide our journeys. When faced with obstacles, let kindness narrate our stories and fortitude sustain our spirits. The world we shape requires rallying around hope in collaboration, knowing our choices are seeds sown into fertile ground—seeds that will bloom in ways we cannot fathom.

Let us be conscious crafters of our legacy, ensuring those who follow inherit stories of hope, resilience, and strength. Collectively, may we embrace choice as a tapestry woven with love and compassion, stitched with lessons learned. Carrying this understanding forward, we become authors not just of our tales but of a resplendent future where each choice is a hopeful note in an unfolding symphony, resonating through the ages with the impact of a thousand harmonies.

Thank You for Joining!

I grew up as the youngest of three in the great Lone Star State. My brother and sister liked to say I was spoiled, but I prefer to think my parents saved the best for last. We were a middle-class Texas family, and for the most part, I've lived a pretty normal life.

Now, at 70 years old, I've been given a gift from God. As I reflect on my life, He's given me one powerful word: CHOICE. I've come to realize that not all my decisions have been wise—and some of them were shaped by choices my parents made before me. This realization hit me like a divine wake-up call. In that moment, God placed it on my heart to write this book and share my journey with you.

This is my assignment, and I've completed it—for Him.

Our Choices shape our lives and the lives of those around us. So choose wisely. Choose the path that walks with Jesus.

P.I.

www.ingramcontent.com/pod-product-compliance
Lightning Source LLC
Chambersburg PA
CBHW051258120626
46547CB00015B/1999